⊕ *BARTHOLOMEW*

Children's Atlas
of the
WORLD

THIS EDITION PRODUCED EXCLUSIVELY FOR
GALLEY PRESS

ISBN 0 86136 761 8

Published in this edition by Galley Press, an imprint of
W.H. Smith and Son Limited, registered no. 237811 England.
Trading as WHS Distributors, St John's House,
East Street, Leicester, LE1 6NE.
Printed in Scotland by John Bartholomew & Son Ltd.

Contents

Introduction

This atlas provides an opportunity for the whole family to learn how to use maps and find out about the world in which they live. The youngest children will use the book with the guidance of a parent or older brother or sister. However, the simple explanations of scale, map terminology and symbols make it suitable for use by most children on their own.

By imaginative use of illustrations and photographs the reader is shown the relationship between the map and reality. Map symbols are also clearly explained.

On pages 10-16 there are examples of British environmental maps and the symbols used on them. These maps cover Towns and cities, Farms, Woods and forests, Moorlands and Mountains. On each page are some illustrations of the different kinds of environment and of plants and other wildlife which may be found in the type of area described.

The next section (pages 17-34) covers the British Isles and the continents in the same environmental map style. The maps covering the rest of Europe and the other continents have been supplemented by information on the people, animals and food of these countries. These maps have been kept simple and uncluttered for ease of reading. The use of hill shading and colour to represent vegetation and land use is the mark of these environmental maps; it gives a realistic impression of what an area is actually like.

Having looked at the world in small sections, in the next few pages (35-43) we bring the continents together and show the full extent of the oceans. If a globe is used in conjunction with these maps, children will see for themselves something of the problem faced by all mapmakers in 'flattening out' the world. When this is done some distortion of size or shape occurs so that, for example, Greenland often appears to be as large as Australia.

The world maps are used to show climate and population distribution. The climatic map divides the world into five temperature zones with superimposed rainfall distribution and is presented in a way that children can readily understand.

Thematic maps (pages 44-57) of the British Isles on Homes, Cities, Power, Climate, Food, Holidays and Travel continue the exploration of our own environment. Single topics are covered in greater detail and illustrated on small scale maps. This section is likely to be of more interest to the older members of the family since it introduces more complex information. The maps are supplemented by pictures and detailed text.

The last section (pages 58-63) on the Moon, Universe and Solar System completes this small, yet comprehensive, family reference book.

Here is a picture of Jane's felt pen.
This is its real size.
It is 10 cm long.

One picture pen is the same size as
one real pen.
We say that the **scale** of the picture pen
is **one to one** (1:1).

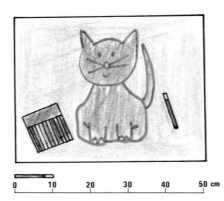

This is a picture of Jane's pens and paper.
They are too big to draw at their real size.
We have drawn them smaller.

Jane has **ten** felt pens.
Use your ruler to find
the length of one of her pens.
Now put your ruler along this scale line.
What is the real length of this pen?

One real pen is as long as
the **ten** picture pens.

In this picture
the **scale is one to ten** (1:10).

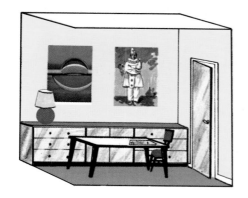

This is a **picture** of Jane's room.
Her pens and paper are on the table.
They are drawn even smaller,
and we can see the whole room.

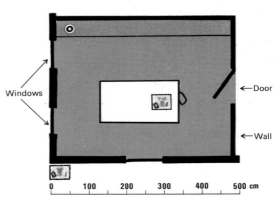

This is a **map** of Jane's room.
Put your ruler along Jane's drawing paper.
Is it 0.5 cm long?
Now put your ruler along the scale line.
Is the paper really 50 cm long?
The **scale** of the map is
one to one hundred (1:100).
What is the real length of Jane's table?

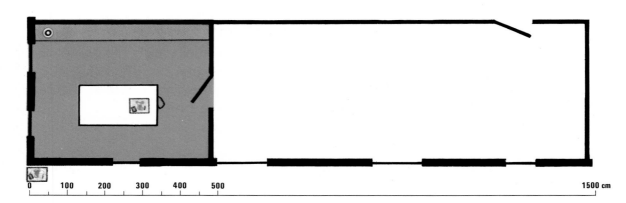

This is the map of Jane's room again.
Has the scale changed?
Look at the room next to Jane's.
How long is it?
How wide is it?

Now draw a map of your
room at home
or of your classroom.

This is where Jane lives.
She lives in a flat in a big house.
To be able to see the whole house
we have had to draw Jane's room
smaller still.
We have measured the pens and paper
at scale 1:1 and scale 1:10.
They are now too small
to be measured accurately.

Maps are drawn at different scales.
To find out about things like
distances and areas on the map
you must know at what scale
the map has been drawn.

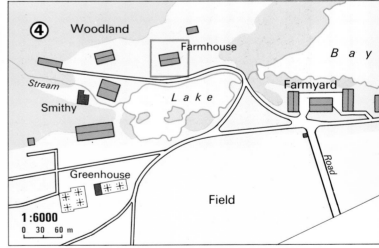

Here is a photograph of the house.
Can you find Jane's room?
Can Jane see the lake
from the room next to hers?

This photograph of the house
was taken from an aeroplane.
You can see more.
Everything looks smaller.
It is at a smaller scale.

This photograph was taken
when the aeroplane flew over the lake.
You can see right down on top of everything.
Can you find the house?

This is a **map** of what was seen
from the aeroplane.
How long is the house?
(20, 30 or 60 metres).

Buildings		Farmland
Roads		Moorland
Water		Woodland

4 Map Scale

Photo: scale 1:10 000

0 100 200 300 400 500

Here is another photograph taken from an aeroplane. It shows the centre of Edinburgh. Find the castle and the station on the street plan. Now find them on the photograph.

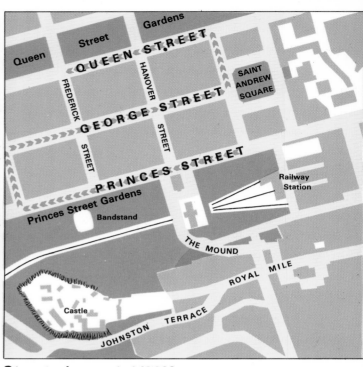

Street plan: scale 1:10 000

(1 km) 1000   (1.5 km) 1500   1900 m

This map shows the same area. The scale of the map is 1:10 000 (one to ten thousand). The red route shows how far Jane walked in one hour. Which streets did she walk along?

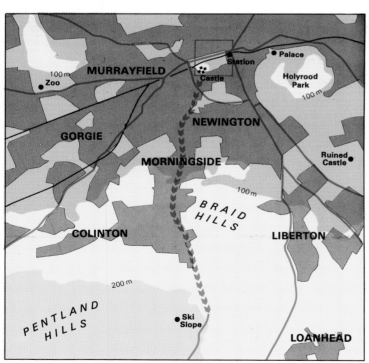

Topographic map: scale 1:100 000

0 1 2 3 4 5 6 km.

Find the red box on the map. It shows the same area as the street plan. This map is at a smaller scale. It took Jane one hour to cycle from the castle to the ski slope.

Motoring map: scale 1:1 000 000

0 10 20 30 34 km.

This is an even smaller map. The scale is 10 times smaller. Jane's father used this map when he took her to Peebles. It took them one hour to get there by car.

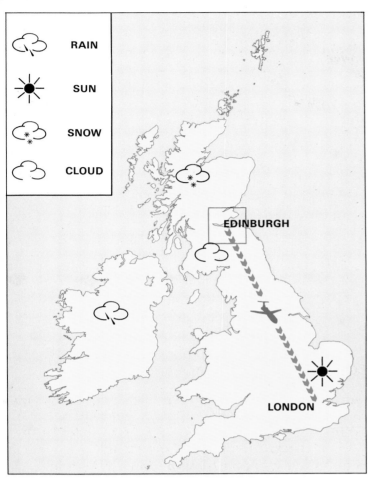

Thematic map: **scale 1:10 000 000**

This is a weather map like those we see on the television. It takes one hour to fly from Edinburgh to London. Is the weather the same in London as in Edinburgh?

Environmental map: **scale 1:100 000 000**

We need a really small scale map to show one of the routes flown by Concorde.
One hour after leaving London it is over Italy.
When you fly in a Concorde you can see the main environments: farmlands, forests, deserts.
Can you see the yellow farmland on the map?

Environment globe

The globe shows the world like a ball.
This is its true shape.
The area of the Environmental map is inside the red line.

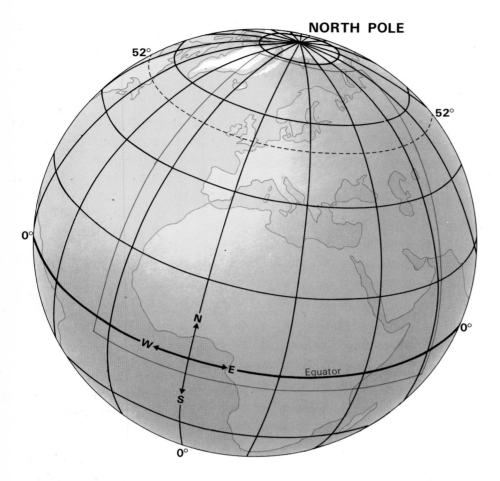

NORTH POLE

52°

52°

0°

0°

0°

N

W

E

S

Equator

Here is a larger globe.
The area in the red box
is the same area as shown
on the globe on Page 5.
Can you find the British Isles
on the globe?

When you play
with a top
it spins round
like this.

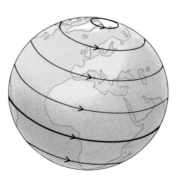

The world also spins.
It turns right round
once every day.
We say it **rotates.**

We can draw lines
from the North Pole
to the South Pole.
We call them
lines of **longitude.**

We can draw lines
running round the world.
We call them
lines of **latitude.**

Lines of longitude and
latitude make a **grid**.
We can use the grid
to find where places are.

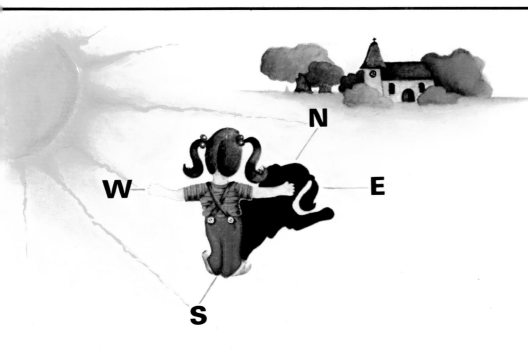

Jane is looking
at the church clock.
It is 12 o'clock midday and
the sun is at its highest
behind her.

When she holds her hands out
her shadow is like a compass.
She is facing **north.**
Her back is towards the **south.**
Her right arm is pointing **east.**
In which direction
is her left arm pointing?

This is how the sun
helps people find
their way about.

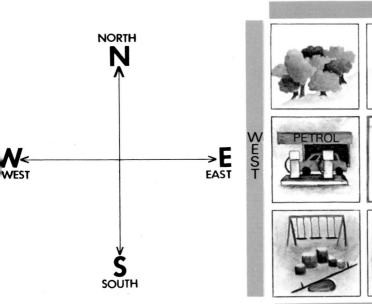

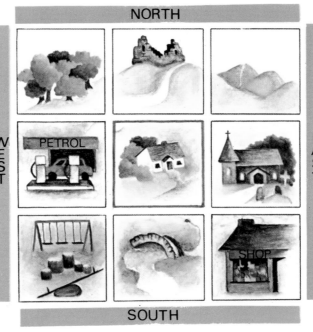

We can also use
direction to find
our way about
on a map or plan.

One has to move North
to get from the house
to the castle.

In what direction do we
have to go to get from:

a) the shop to the hills?
b) the hills to the castle?
c) the castle to the river?

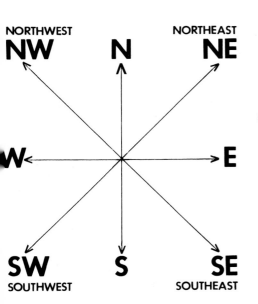

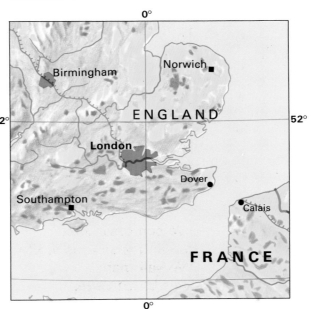

Not all directions are
exactly, North, East,
South or West.

Some other directions
are Northeast, Southeast,
Southwest, and
Northwest.

In which direction
does Jane go to get:

a) from London to
   Birmingham?
b) from Dover to Calais?

This is part of Wales.
The high parts
have been coloured brown.
How many hill tops can you count?
Now find this area
on the bigger map on page 9.
Look at the key.
What colour has been used
for the low parts?

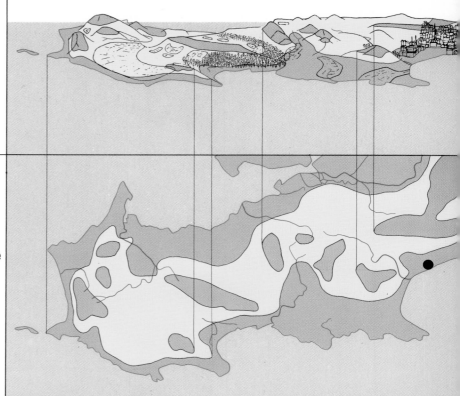

Here is the map of this part of Wales.
Maps that show how high the land
is are called **relief maps.**

What can you see in the picture above
that is not shown on this relief map?

There are even higher areas on the
relief map on page 9. Can you find
them? How are roads shown on this
map?

This is the same part of Wales.
It is the view we would see
from an aeroplane.
We can see
the proper shape of the land.
Now find this area
on the bigger map on page 9.
Look at the key.
What colours have been used
for towns, arable land and
woodland?

Here is another map
of this part of Wales.
How are roads shown on the map on
page 9? The hills and valleys
can be seen more clearly.
Town, farm and forest are also shown.
These are called environments.
A map that shows environments
is called an **environmental map.**

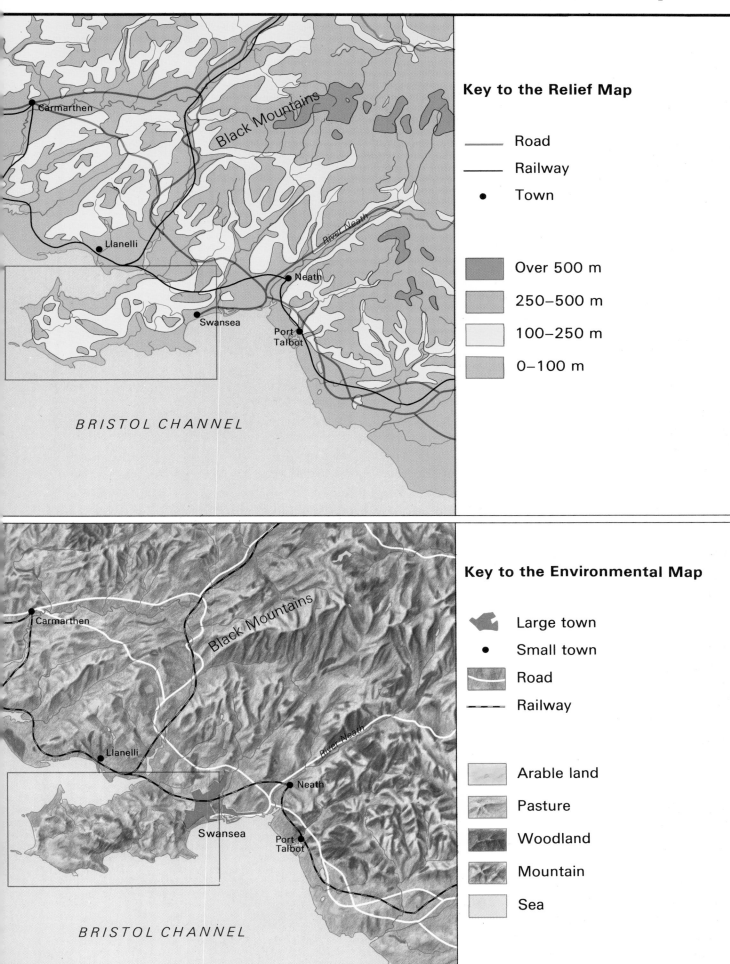

Key to the Relief Map

——— Road

——— Railway

• Town

Over 500 m

250–500 m

100–250 m

0–100 m

Key to the Environmental Map

Large town

• Small town

Road

Railway

Arable land

Pasture

Woodland

Mountain

Sea

Urban
area

Most families live and work
in towns and cities.
These are called **urban areas.**
The largest urban areas are on
the map. The box of colour
above the map tells us that on
the main maps in this atlas
urban areas will be shown in red.

Can you see where people
work in the photograph and
where they live in the picture?
What does the land at the
edge of the town get used for?
The change from one
environment to the next usually
happens very gradually.

Arable
land

At the edge of the urban environment we start to move into the farming environment. The land which is ploughed and cropped is called **arable land.** Is it found mainly on the east side or west side of Britain?

In the picture a grain crop is being harvested.
The yellow colour of ripe grain is used on the maps in this atlas to show arable land.
Lots of animals and wild plants live along the edges of fields.
How many can you recognise?

Pasture

Some farms keep herds of animals instead of growing crops.
Land used for feeding animals is called **pasture.**
What colour will be used to show pasture on our maps?

Make a list of the farm animals you see in the picture.
What other animals have made their homes here?

Woodland

Woodland areas are spread across the country as you can see on the map.
This environment is rich in the variety of plants and animals which live here.

You may have seen a deer or brambles before.
See if you can find out the names of some of the other woodland plants and animals.

Moorland

Moors are usually found on high ground.
Only plants that can live in these cold, wet and windy conditions are found here. Which ones can you see in the picture?

Look at where the moors are on the map.
Find out why the moors and heaths are to be found in these areas.

Mountain

Use the map to find the few areas where this **high mountain** environment exists. The photograph shows that this environment is extremely cold and that there is little soil for plants to grow.

The few plants and animals that live here find shelter between the rocks from this harsh environment. How does man use or enjoy this environment?

Coast

Road

River

Railway

Canal

 Urban area

 Arable land

 Improved grassland

 Woodland

 Moorland – unimproved grassland

 Mountain

 International boundary

 National boundary

Lake

0　100　200 km

1 cm = 50 km

1:5 000 000

A　10°　B　5°　C　0°　D

①

Shetland

60°

Orkney

John O'Groats

②

ATLANTIC

OCEAN

Hebrides

Skye

North West Highlands

SCOTLAND

Grampians

Aberdeen

Ben Nevis

NORTH

SEA

Edinburgh

Glasgow

Southern Uplands

55°

Newcastle

NORTHERN

LOUGH NEAGH

IRELAND

Belfast

Pennines

UNITED KINGDOM

REPUBLIC OF

IRELAND

IRISH SEA

Hull

Liverpool

Manchester

Dublin

River Shannon

Cambrian Mountains

Norwich

③

Birmingham

WALES

ENGLAND

River Thames

Cork

River Severn

Cardiff

Bristol

London

Dover

CELTIC

Southampton

Calais

SEA

Isle of

Wight

Land's End

CHANNEL

50°

Isles of Scilly

ENGLISH

CHANNEL ISLANDS

FRANCE

④

B　5°　C　0°

Isles
of Scilly

50°

52°

③

④

⑤

B

C

D

E

Land's End
St. Ives
Lizard Pt.
Falmouth
Plymouth
DARTMOOR
Torquay
Ilfracombe
EXMOOR

BRISTOL CHANNEL

Milford Haven
Fishguard
CARDIGAN BAY
Aberystwyth
Barmouth
Cambrian Mountains
Swansea
Newport
Cardiff
Weston
Bath
Bristol
River Severn
COTSWOLDS
Birmingham
Wolverhampton
Stratford-upon-Avon
Coventry
Leicester
Peterborough
THE FENS
Cambridge
Thetford
Norwich
Great Yarmouth
Ipswich
Harwich
Southend
Tilbury
Epping
River Ouse
River Thames
London
Windsor
Reading
Oxford
Luton
Milton Keynes
Northampton
Guildford
Brighton
Hastings
Dungeness
Dover
Margate
STRAIT OF DOVER
Calais
Boulogne
SALISBURY PLAIN
Portland Bill
Bournemouth
New Forest
Southampton
Portsmouth
ISLE OF WIGHT

ENGLISH CHANNEL

CHANNEL ISLANDS
Guernsey
Alderney
Sark
Jersey
Cherbourg
Le Havre
Dieppe
Rouen
FRANCE

4°
0°
2°

0   50 km

1 cm = 20 km

A **B** **C** **D** **E**

Colonsay
Mull
Jura
Oban
Islay
Mull of Kintyre
Arran
FIRTH OF CLYDE
Bute
NORTH CHANNEL
Ayr
Glasgow
Cumbernauld
LOCH LOMOND
River Forth
Stirling
Perth
Dundee
St Andrews
FIRTH OF FORTH
Edinburgh
River Clyde
Peebles
S C O T L A N D
Southern Uplands
Galashiels
River Tweed
Hawick
Berwick

Dublin
Dún Laoghaire
Belfast
NORTHERN IRELAND
Larne
Stranraer

I R I S H   S E A
ISLE OF MAN
Douglas
Mourne Mountains

Holyhead
Anglesey
Caernarfon
1085 Mount Snowdon
Colwyn Bay

SOLWAY FIRTH
Dumfries
Carlisle
C h e v i o t s
Keswick
Cumbrian Mountains
.977 Scafell Pike
LAKE WINDERMERE
Morecambe
Blackpool
Southport
Blackburn
Bolton
Liverpool
Manchester
Crewe
Stoke
Nottingham
Sheffield
Huddersfield
Bradford
Leeds
York
River Tees
NORTH YORK MOORS
Middlesbrough
Sunderland
Newcastle
River Tyne

Scarborough
Hull
Humber
River Trent
Grimsby

N O R T H   S E A
THE

Environment

54°
54°
56°
56°
6°
4°
2°
0°

Fair Isle

ORKNEY

Kirkwall

PENTLAND FIRTH

John'o Groats

Wick

SHETLAND

Lerwick

Fair Isle

Cape Wrath

Stornoway

Lewis

THE MINCH

Harris

MORAY FIRTH

Banff

North Uist

Peterhead

Hebrides

Skye

Inverness

North West Highlands

LOCH NESS

River Spey

South Uist

Aviemore

River Don

Aberdeen

Rum

Cairngorms

River Dee

Eigg

Ardnamurchan Point

Ben Nevis
1344

Fort William

Coll

G r a m p i a n s

River Tay

Tiree

Mull

Oban

Dundee

Iona

Perth

St. Andrews

Colonsay

River Forth

Jura

Stirling

FIRTH OF FORTH

LOCH LOMOND

Cumbernauld

Edinburgh

Islay

Glasgow

Bute

River Clyde

Berwick

Arran

Peebles

Galashiels

River Tweed

Mull of Kintyre

Southern Uplands

Ayr

Hawick

Cheviots

FIRTH OF CLYDE

NORTH CHANNEL

Dumfries

Newcastle

NORTHERN IRELAND

Stranraer

Carlisle

River Tyne

Sunderla

SOLWAY FIRTH

E N G L A N D

Belfast

0   50 km

1 cm = 20 km

Glasgow
more than 500 000 inhabitants

Nottingham
250 000–500 000 inhabitants

Dundee
100 000–250 000 inhabitants

● Carlisle
25 000–100 000 inhabitants

• Berwick
less than 25 000 inhabitants

International boundary
National boundary
County/region boundary
Railway
Motorway and major road
Other road
Canal
• 1041 Height in metres

Environment

Mountain
Moorland, Unimproved grassland
Improved grassland
Arable land
Woodland
Built-up area

ATLANTIC OCEAN

DONEGAL BAY

Malin Head
Donegal
Sligo
Castlebar

Galway
GALWAY BAY
Aran Islands

Shannon
River Shannon
Limerick

Tralee
Killarney
DINGLE BAY
1041
Carrauntoohill
Bantry
BANTRY BAY
Mizen Head

Cork

Tipperary

Waterford

Wexford

IRELAND

REPUBLIC OF

Athlone
BOG OF ALLEN
LOUGH REE
LOUGH DERG

River Boyne
Hill of Tara

River Liffey

Dublin
Dún Laoghaire

Wicklow Mountains

Wicklow

Omagh
LOWER LOUGH ERNE
UPPER LOUGH ERNE

Cavan

NORTHERN

IRELAND

Londonderry
LOUGH FOYLE
Portrush
Giant's Causeway
Rathlin Island
River Bann
LOUGH NEAGH
Armagh
Newry
Dundalk
Mourne Mountains

Larne
Belfast
River Lagan
Downpatrick

Islay
Arran
SCOTLAND
Stranraer

NORTH CHANNEL

ISLE OF MAN

IRISH SEA

ST. GEORGE'S CHANNEL

Fishguard
WALES

A B C D
1
2
3
4

The large map shows
the continent of Europe.
Find Europe on the globe.
Is Europe larger or smaller
than Asia?
Which three countries in Europe
would you like to go to for a holiday?
Use the map and pictures
to find out more about Europe.

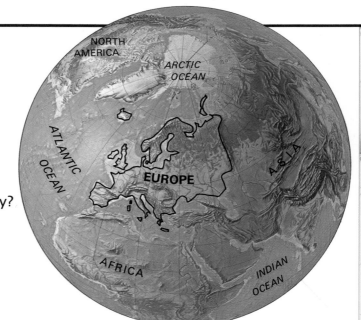

Which children live in Europe?

Slavonic

British   Mediterranean   Nordic

What is a favourite food in Denmark?

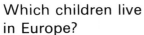

1 Smorrebrod   2 Wine   3 Pizza
4 Pork pie   5 Sausage

Name a country where lizards are very common.

Golden eagle   Red deer   Badger

Lizard   Grey seal

Scale 0 500 1000 km

1 cm = 200 km

1:20 000 000

23

ARCTIC OCEAN
Spitsbergen

D E F G H J K L M N O P Q R S T U V W X Y

BARENTS SEA

North Cape

NORWEGIAN SEA

Lofoten

Arctic Circle

Faeroes

Shetland

Orkney

Aberdeen NORTH SEA

UNITED
KINGDOM

Edinburgh

Belfast

Dublin

Cardiff
Birmingham

London

ENGLISH CHANNEL

NETHER-
LANDS

Amsterdam

BELGIUM

Brussels

LUXEM-
BOURG

BRITTANY

Bonn

WEST
GERMANY

Paris

FRANCE

Bordeaux

R.Garonne

Seine

River Loire

Marseille

MONACO

ANDORRA

Pyrenees

Barcelona

Corsica

Sardinia

Majorca

Algiers

Tunis

ALGERIA

TUNISIA

Tripoli

NORWAY

Bergen

Oslo

SWEDEN

Stockholm

Gothenburg

LAKE
VÄNERN

SKAGERRAK

DENMARK

Copenhagen

BALTIC SEA

GULF OF BOTHNIA

FINLAND

Helsinki

LAPLAND

Kola
Peninsula

WHITE SEA

LAKE
LADOGA

LAKE
ONEGA

Leningrad

Berlin

EAST
GERMANY

Prague

River Elbe

River Oder

Warsaw

POLAND

River Vistula

CZECHOSLOVAKIA

Vienna

Bern

SWITZERLAND

Mont
Blanc 4807

The Alps

Milan

Venice

ITALY

Rome

Naples

Mount
Vesuvius

Sicily

Mount Etna

MALTA
Valletta

MEDITERRANEAN SEA

Benghazi

LIBYA

AUSTRIA

Budapest

HUNGARY

Carpathians

ROMANIA

Bucharest

Belgrade

YUGOSLAVIA

River Danube

Sofia

BULGARIA

Tirana

ALBA-
NIA

ADRIATIC SEA

AEGEAN
SEA

GREECE

Athens

Crete

Rhodes

Istanbul

Ankara

TURKEY

ANATOLIA

Taurus Mountains

Nicosia

CYPRUS

SOVIET

UNION

Moscow

Gorki

River Volga

Kuybyshev

Ural Mountains

North Dvina River

Novaya
Zemlya

KARA
SEA

Yamal
Peninsula

Arctic Circle

River Dnieper

Kiev

Kharkov

UKRAINE

Odessa

Crimea

Rostov

River Don

BLACK SEA

Alexandria

Nile Delta

EGYPT

Cairo

Mountains

Key

More than 5 000 000 inhabitants

1 000 000 – 5 000 000 inhabitants

Less than 1 000 000 inhabitants

International boundary

Disputed international boundary

Other boundary

Canal

•4807 Height in metres

Arable land

Pasture

Steppe

Desert

Tundra

Coniferous forest

Deciduous forest

Glacier

The large map shows
the continent of Asia.
Find Asia on the map.
Find Asia on the globe.
Which continents are next to Asia?
Which are the three largest
countries in Asia?
Use the map and pictures
to find out more about Asia.

Do Arab children live in
deserts or in forests?

Name a food eaten by
Russian boys and girls.

What animals live in Asia?

Chinese
Russian
Indian
Arab

1 Kebabs
2 Seafood
3 Rice
4 Rye bread
5 Curry

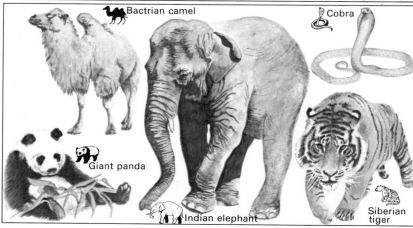

Bactrian camel
Cobra
Giant panda
Indian elephant
Siberian tiger

Key

	More than 5 000 0 inhabitants
	1 000 000–5 000 0 inhabitants
	Less than 1 000 00 inhabitants
——	International boundary
---	Disputed interna-tional boundary
——	Other boundary
⊔⊔⊔	Canal
•8848	Height in metres

0 500 1000 km

1 cm = 400 km

1:40 000 000

60° 70° 80° 80° 70° 60° 3

ATLANTIC
OCEAN

ARCTIC
OCEAN

BERING STRAIT

170°

Chukotsk
Peninsula

BERING
SEA

180°

NORWAY
Oslo
SWEDEN
Stockholm
FINLAND
Helsinki
Leningrad

Spitsbergen

Franz Josef
Land

Novaya
Zemlya

Severnaya
Zemlya

New Siberian
Islands

Wrangel
Island

Kamchatka

170°

BARENTS
SEA

KARA SEA

Taymyr Peninsula

Dikson

Verkhoyansk Mountains

SEA OF
OKHOTSK

160°

TIC SEA

WHITE SEA

Yamal
Peninsula

Arkhangel'sk

River Ob

River Yenisey

Arctic Circle

River Lena

Yakutsk

Sakhalin

4

150°

Kiev
Kharkov

Moscow

S I B E R I A

Stanovoy Mountains

River Amur

Ural Mountains

Sverdlovsk

S O V I E T   U N I O N

River Volga

Magnitogorsk

Novosibirsk

LAKE
BAYKAL

River Ural

KIRGHIZ STEPPE

MANCHURIA

Vladivostok

SEA OF
JAPAN

JAPAN
Tokyo

5

Baku

CASPIAN
SEA

ARAL SEA

LAKE
BALKHASH

Ulan Bator

MONGOLIA

NORTH
KOREA
Pyongyang

Shenyang

Fujiyama

140°

Caucasus

KARA KUM

Tashkent

GOBI

Peking

Seoul
SOUTH
KOREA

Osaka

Zagros Mountains

Tehran

Tien Shan

YELLOW
SEA

Nagasaki

IRAN

AFGHANISTAN
Kabul

Islamabad

Kunlun Shan

C H I N A

Hwang Ho

Shanghai

6

AHRAIN
GULF
TAR

Karachi

KASHMIR

TIBET

RED
BASIN

Chungking

Yangtze Kiang

EAST CHINA SEA

Taipei

Tropic of Cancer

PAKISTAN

Delhi

H i m a l a y a s

Wuhan

NITED
RAB
MIRATES
Muscat
OMAN

New Delhi

NEPAL
Katmandu

Mount
Everest
8848

BHUTAN

Brahmaputra R.

NAN LING

Canton

TAIWAN

GULF OF OMAN

River Ganges

BANGLA-
DESH
Dacca

River Irrawaddy

HONG
KONG
MACAO

I N D I A

Calcutta

7

130°

ARABIAN
SEA

Bombay

DECCAN

Hyderabad

BAY OF

BENGAL

Andaman
Islands

BURMA

Rangoon

LAOS

Vientiane

River Mekong

Hanoi

VIETNAM

SOUTH CHINA SEA

Manila

PHILIPPINES

THAILAND
Bangkok

Laccadive
Islands

Madras

CAMBODIA
Phnom
Penh

Ho Chi Minh
City

8

Cape
Comorin

SRI LANKA
Colombo

Nicobar
Islands

GULF OF
THAILAND

BRUNEI

MALAYSIA

MALDIVES

Equator

MALAYSIA
Kuala
Lumpur

STRAIT OF MALACCA

Sumatra

SINGAPORE

Borneo

Sulawesi

9

INDIAN
OCEAN

JAVA SEA

INDONESIA

Jakarta
Java

K 90° L 100° M 110° N 120° O

Legend

- Arable land
- Pasture
- Savanna
- Steppe
- Desert
- Tundra
- Coniferous forest
- Deciduous forest
- Rain forest
- Glacier

The large map shows the continent of Africa.
Find Africa on the globe.
Name the oceans around Africa.
What is the large desert called?
Use the map and pictures
to find out more about Africa.

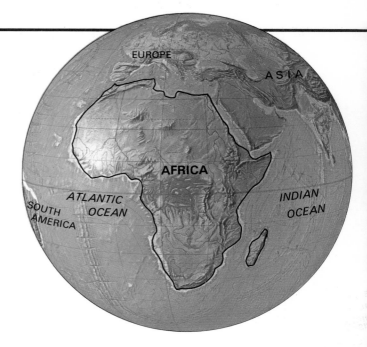

Do pygmy boys and girls
live in deserts or in forests?

Name five foods eaten in Africa.

What is the name of the big river
where crocodiles live?

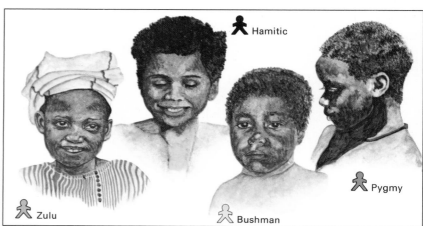

Hamitic

Pygmy

Zulu

Bushman

1 Sweet Potato

2 Cooked leaves

3 Date

5 Bananas

4 Corn

Rhino

Antelope

Crocodile

Gorilla

Lion

0 500 1000 km

1 cm = 400 km

1:40 000 000

20° 40° (A) 10° (B) 0° (C) 10° (D) 20° (E) 30° (F) 40° (G) 50° (H) 40° 60°

PORTUGAL SPAIN ITALY TURKEY ①

Madeira GREECE ②

Casablanca Rabat GIBRALTAR Algiers Tunis MALTA CYPRUS SYRIA River Euphrates Baghdad IRAN 30°

Canary Islands MOROCCO Atlas Mountains TUNISIA MEDITERRANEAN SEA LEBANON Damascus IRAQ

Benghazi Tripoli ISRAEL Amman KUWAIT ②

ALGERIA LIBYA EGYPT Alexandria Jerusalem JORDAN Kuwait BAHRAIN QATAR Muscat

Tropic of Cancer Cairo Suez Canal Sinai River Nile SAUDI Riyadh UNITED ARAB EMIRATES OMAN

MAURITANIA S A H A R A LAKE NASSER ARABIA Mecca RUB AL KHALI 20°

Nouakchott MALI YEMEN SOUTH YEMEN ③

SENEGAL Timbuktu Sana Aden GULF OF ADEN Socotra

Dakar River Senegal NIGER CHAD Khartoum DJIBOUTI Djibouti

GAMBIA Bamako River Niger Niamey LAKE CHAD SUDAN Blue Nile 10°

Bissau UPPER Ouagadougou N'Djamena Addis Ababa ETHIOPIA ④

GUINEA VOLTA NIGERIA White Nile SOMALIA

Conakry SIERRA GHANA CENTRAL Mogadishu

Freetown LEONE IVORY TOGO BENIN AFRICAN REPUBLIC UGANDA LAKE Equator 0°

Monrovia COAST LAKE Lagos Bangui Yaoundé Kampala RUDOLF Nairobi INDIAN

LIBERIA Abidjan VOLTA River Niger CAMEROON River Zaire KENYA Mount SEYCHELLES

Accra Lomé Malabo Stanley Falls RWANDA Kilimanjaro Mombasa OCEAN

Porto Novo EQUATORIAL Libreville Kigali LAKE 5895 ⑤

GULF GUINEA River Congo CONGO ZAIRE BURUNDI VICTORIA Bujumbura TANZANIA

OF GUINEA SÃO TOMÉ GABON Brazzaville Kinshasa Great LAKE Dar es Salaam

& PRINCIPE CABINDA TANGANYIKA Rift COMORO

ATLANTIC Luanda Valley ISLANDS ⑥

OCEAN ANGOLA MALAWI LAKE

River Cubango ZAMBIA NYASA Lilongwe Antananarivo MAURITIUS

A 10° B 0° C River Zambezi Lusaka MOZAMBIQUE Réunion

Key Victoria Harare Beira MADAGASCAR

More than 5 000 000 inhabitants Falls ZIMBABWE Tropic of Capricorn

1 000 000 – 5 000 000 inhabitants NAMIBIA (RHODESIA)

Less than 1 000 000 inhabitants BOTSWANA

International boundary WALVIS BAY KALAHARI Pretoria Maputo

Disputed international boundary (S.W. AFRICA) DESERT Gaborone Mbabane SWAZILAND

Canal Johannesburg INDIAN ⑦

Waterfall River Orange Maseru LESOTHO

• 5895 Height in metres SOUTH High Veld Durban 30°

AFRICA

Arable land Cape Town Port Elizabeth OCEAN

Pasture Cape of Good Hope ⑧

Savanna

Steppe

Desert

Rain forest

Other forest

10° D 20° E 30° F 40° G 50° 50° H 60° 40°

The large map shows
the continent of North America.
Find North America on the globe.
The North Pole is between North America
and another continent. Which is it?
What part of the United States (America)
is next to the Soviet Union (Russia)?
Use the map and pictures
to find out more about North America.

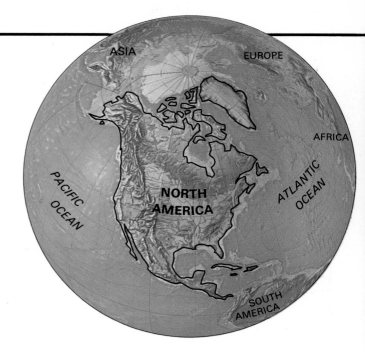

Which children live in North America?

White American

Red Indian

Eskimo

American Negro

Name a food that is popular in Mexico.

1 Hamburger

2 Salmon

5 Fruit basket

4 Tortillas

3 Water melon

Are rattlesnakes common
in Canada or in the USA?

Alligator

Bison

Beaver

Rattlesnake

Caribou

0 500 1000 km

1 cm = 400 km

1:40 000 000

③ ② ① ⓐ ① ②
ALASKA

BERING STRAIT BEAUFORT SEA

ⓐ ⓑ ⓒ ⓓ ⓔ ⓕ

GREENLAND

① Ⓠ ②
Reykjavík ICELAND

Thule Arctic Circle

Queen Elizabeth
Islands

Banks
Island

Ⓟ

Ⓞ

Godthåb ③

ⓖ Victoria Ⓗ ⓙ Ⓚ Ⓛ Ⓜ Ⓝ
Island

Baffin Island

DAVIS STRAIT

Yukon River 6194 Mount
McKinley
Anchorage

GULF OF
ALASKA

Aleutian Islands

Mackenzie River

GREAT BEAR
LAKE

GREAT SLAVE
LAKE

HUDSON
BAY

C A N A D A

LABRADOR

Newfoundland

St. John's ④

Churchill

Edmonton

Calgary Saskatoon

Vancouver
Island Vancouver

Seattle

ROCKY MOUNTAINS

LAKE
WINNIPEG

Winnipeg

Missouri River

LAKE
SUPERIOR

Quebec

Montreal

Ottawa LAKE HURON Toronto
LAKE MICHIGAN Niagara St. Lawrence River
Falls

Halifax

⑤

San Francisco

Sierra Nevada

Los Angeles

GREAT
SALT LAKE
GREAT
BASIN

UNITED STATES

Denver

Colorado River OF AMERICA

GRAND
CANYON

P R A I R I E S

Detroit LAKE ERIE New York
Chicago Philadelphia
Washington

Appalachian Mountains Boston

ATLANTIC

Bermuda

PACIFIC

OCEAN

Lower California

Rio Grande

Dallas

Houston

New
Orleans

Mississippi River Ohio River

Florida Cape Canaveral

GULF OF MEXICO Miami

OCEAN ⑥

Tropic of Cancer

Nassau
THE BAHAMAS

MEXICO

Havana

CUBA

HAITI DOMINICAN
REPUBLIC

Mexico City

Yucatán

JAMAICA Port-au- Santo
Kingston Prince Domingo

West Indies ⑦

Acapulco

BELIZE
Belmopan

CARIBBEAN SEA

GUATEMALA HONDURAS
Guatemala Tegucigalpa
San Salvador NICARAGUA
EL SALVADOR Managua

Caracas

San José Panamá Canal Panamá VENEZUELA
COSTA RICA PANAMÁ ⑧

Medellín

Bogotá

COLOMBIA

Equator Quito

Galapagos ECUADOR
Islands

⑨

B R A Z I L

PERU

Lima

ⓕ ⓖ ⓗ ⓙ Ⓚ Ⓛ Ⓜ
130° 120° 110° 100° 90° 80° 70°

Key

More than 5 000 000 inhabitants

1 000 000 – 5 000 000 inhabitants

Less than 1 000 000 inhabitants

International boundary

Other boundary

Canal

Waterfall

• 6194 Height in metres

Arable land

Pasture

Steppe

Desert

Tundra

Coniferous forest

Deciduous forest

Rain forest

Glacier

The large map shows
the continent of South America.
Find South America on the globe.
South America is joined to another continent.
Which one is it?
Name the largest country in South America.
Use the map and pictures
to find out more about South America.

In which country do gauchos live?

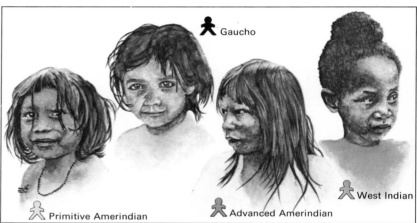

Gaucho

Primitive Amerindian

Advanced Amerindian

West Indian

Which children
sometimes eat flying fish?

1 Flying fish

2 Chili con carne

3 Brazil nut

4 Barbeque

5 Coffee

What animals live in South America?

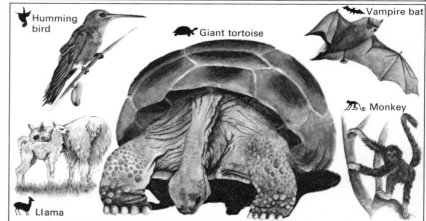

Humming bird

Giant tortoise

Vampire bat

Monkey

Llama

0   500   1000 km

1 cm = 400 km

1:40 000 000

MEXICO

CUBA

BELIZE

GUATEMALA

HONDURAS

EL SALVADOR

NICARAGUA

CARIBBEAN SEA

DOMINICA

ST. LUCIA
ST. VINCENT   BARBADOS
GRENADA

COSTA RICA

PANAMÁ

Caracas   TRINIDAD & TOBAGO

Medellin

VENEZUELA   Georgetown
                              Paramaribo
Bogotá   Cayenne

LLANOS

GUYANA   SURI—
                   NAM   FRENCH
                              GUIANA

COLOMBIA   R. Orinoco

Guiana

ATLANTIC

OCEAN

Tropic of Cancer

Galapagos
Islands

Quito
ECUADOR

Highlands

Rio Negro

River Putumayo

Equator

Iquitos

Manaus   River Amazon

PACIFIC

OCEAN

S E L V A S

River Madeira

River Tapajós

River Xingu

R. Tocantins

Recife

Andes

PERU

C A T I N G A S

B R A Z I L

Lima

LAKE TITICACA

La Paz

BOLIVIA

MATO
GROSSO

CAMPOS

Salvador

River Marañon

Brasilia

Brazilian
Highlands

GRAN CHACO

PARAGUAY

Asunción

Rio de Janeiro
São Paulo

CHILE

Andes

6959
Aconcagua

ARGENTINA

URUGUAY
Montevideo

RIO DE LA PLATA

Tropic of Capricorn

ATLANTIC

Santiago

Buenos Aires

PAMPAS

OCEAN

PATAGONIA

Puerto Montt

Falkland Islands
                Stanley

STRAIT OF
MAGELLAN   Tierra del Fuego

South Georgia

Cape Horn

ANTARCTICA

Key

-  More than 5 000 000 inhabitants
- ■ 1 000 000 – 5 000 000 inhabitants
- ● Less than 1 000 000 inhabitants
- —— International boundary
- Canal
- Waterfall
- •6959 Height in metres

Arable land

Savanna

Steppe

Desert

Rain forest

Other forest

Glacier

The large map shows the continent of Australia.
Find Australia on the globe.
Name the oceans around Australia.
What place has the name of
the explorer Captain James Cook?
Use the map and pictures
to find out more about Australia.

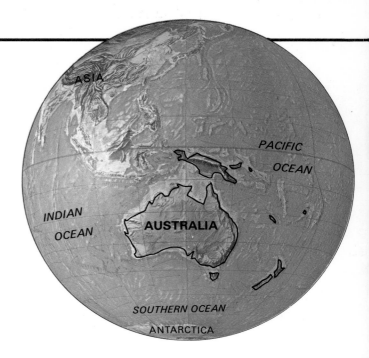

What do we call
the natives in New Zealand?

Name the foods
eaten in this part of the world.

Where are kangaroos found?

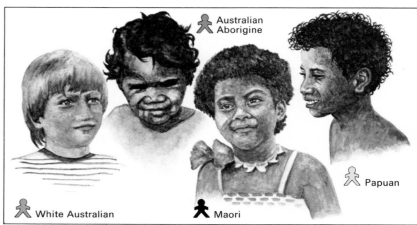

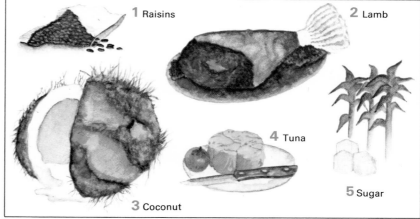

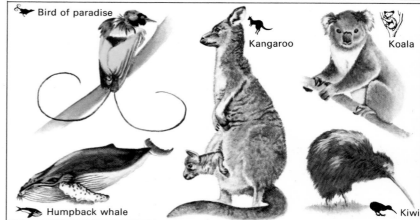

0 500 1000 km

1 cm = 400 km

1:40 000 000

110° Ⓐ 120° Ⓑ 130° Ⓒ 140° Ⓓ 150° Ⓔ 160° Ⓕ 170° Ⓖ 180° Ⓗ

20° ①

Manila

PHILIPPINES

Mariana Islands

P A C I F I C

O C E A N

①

Marshall Islands

②

BRUNEI SABAH

SARAWAK

Caroline Islands

②

Borneo

Celebes

Equator

NAURU

KIRIBATI

0°

INDONESIA

IRIAN JAYA

New Guinea

PAPUA NEW GUINEA

③

SOLOMON ISLANDS

Honiara

TUVALU

③

Timor

ARAFURA SEA

Port Moresby

TIMOR SEA

Darwin

CORAL SEA

VANUATU

④

New Caledonia

FIJI Suva

Great Barrier Reef

TONGA

Tropic of Capricorn

NORTHERN

TERRITORY

GREAT SANDY DESERT

QUEENSLAND

North West Cape

WESTERN AUSTRALIA

GIBSON DESERT

A U S T R A L I A

⑤

Brisbane

GREAT VICTORIA DESERT

LAKE EYRE

SOUTH AUSTRALIA

Kalgoorlie

NEW SOUTH

Darling River

30°

Perth

GREAT

AUSTRALIAN BIGHT

Adelaide

WALES

Sydney

Murray River

2237

Canberra

Australian Alps

VICTORIA

Melbourne

TASMAN SEA

Auckland

NEW ZEALAND

North Island

⑥

BASS STRAIT

TASMANIA

Hobart

South Island

Wellington

Christchurch

40°

Mount Cook

⑦

90° 100° 110° Ⓐ 120° Ⓑ 130° Ⓒ 140° Ⓓ 150° Ⓔ 160° Ⓕ 170° Ⓖ 180°

50°

S O U T H E R N   O C E A N

⑧

60°

Key

■	1 000 000 – 5 000 000 inhabitants
●	Less than 1 000 000 inhabitants
—	International boundary
—	Other boundary

• 2237 Height in metres

Arable land

Pasture

Savanna

Steppe

Desert

Rain forest

Other forest

170°

⑨

170°

160° 150° 140° 130°

70°

1:50 000 000

0   500   1000   1500 km

1 cm = 50 km

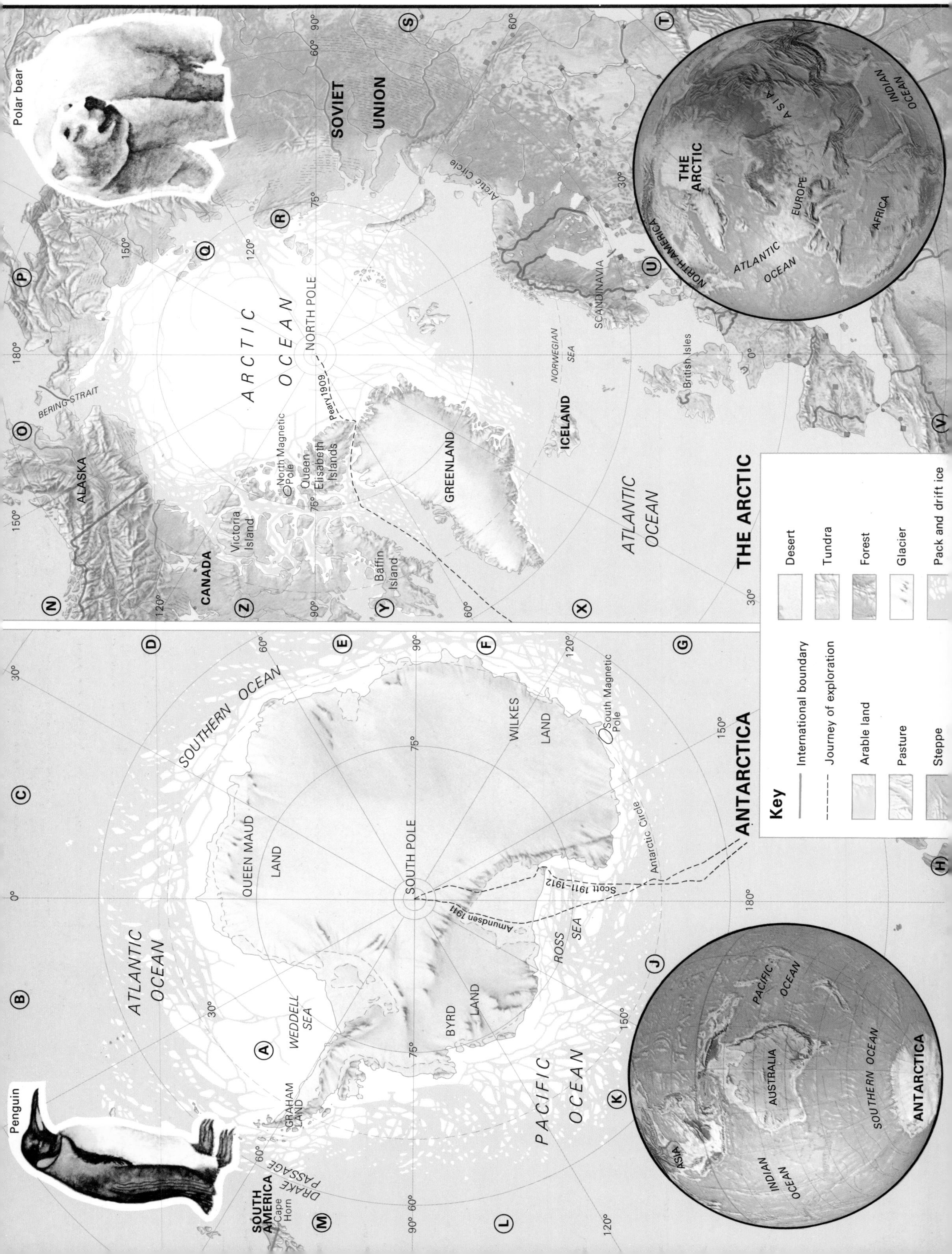

Polar bear

SOVIET

UNION

THE ARCTIC

ASIA

EUROPE

INDIAN
OCEAN

NORTH AMERICA

ATLANTIC
OCEAN

AFRICA

T

S

R

Q

P

O

N

150°

120°

180°

150°

ALASKA

BERING STRAIT

A R C T I C   O C E A N

NORTH POLE

Peary 1909

North Magnetic
Pole

Queen
Elisabeth
Islands

Victoria
Island

CANADA

Baffin
Island

GREENLAND

Arctic Circle

90°

75°

60°

30°

0°

NORWEGIAN
SEA

SCANDINAVIA

British Isles

ICELAND

ATLANTIC
OCEAN

THE ARCTIC

U

V

X

Y

Z

120°

90°

75°

60°

30°

Key

Desert	
Tundra	
Forest	
Glacier	
Pack and drift ice	

International boundary

Journey of exploration

Arable land

Pasture

Steppe

D

E

F

G

C

B

A

M

L

K

J

H

30°

60°

90°

120°

150°

180°

150°

120°

90°

60°

30°

0°

SOUTHERN   OCEAN

WILKES
LAND

South Magnetic
Pole

QUEEN MAUD
LAND

SOUTH POLE

Scott 1911-1912

Amundsen 1911

Antarctic Circle

BYRD
LAND

ROSS
SEA

WEDDELL
SEA

GRAHAM
LAND

SOUTH
AMERICA
Cape
Horn

DRAKE
PASSAGE

ATLANTIC
OCEAN

PACIFIC
OCEAN

ANTARCTICA

ASIA

AUSTRALIA

INDIAN
OCEAN

PACIFIC
OCEAN

SOUTHERN OCEAN

ANTARCTICA

Penguin

75°

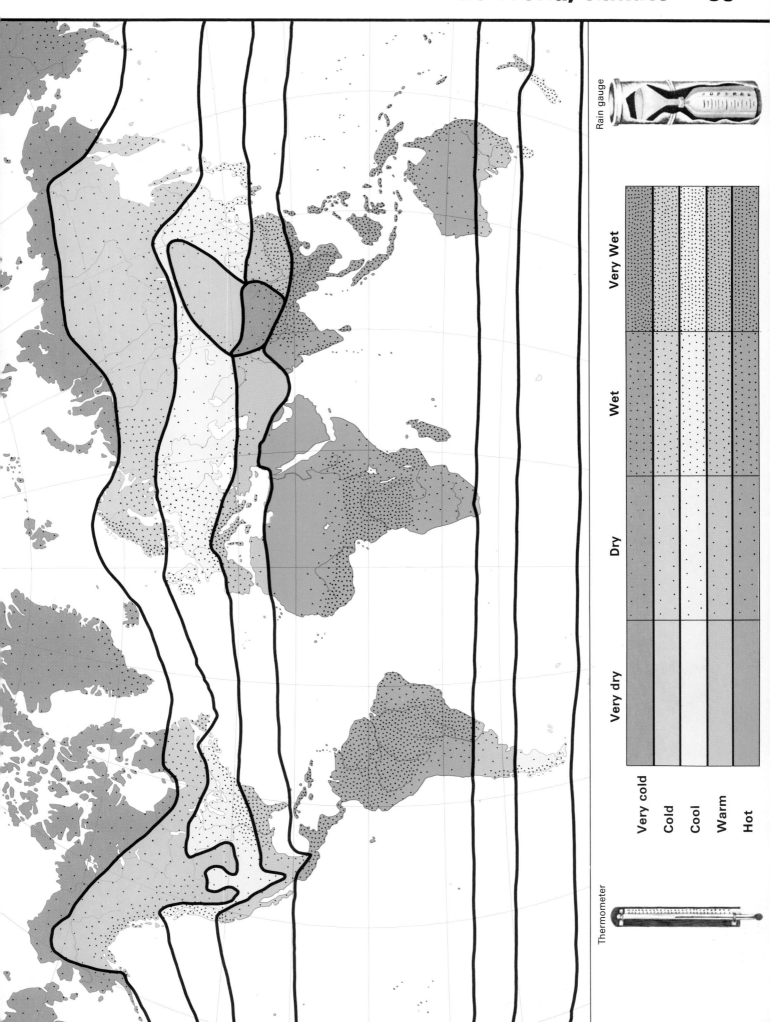

Rain gauge

Very Wet

Wet

Dry

Very dry

Very cold

Cold

Cool

Warm

Hot

Thermometer

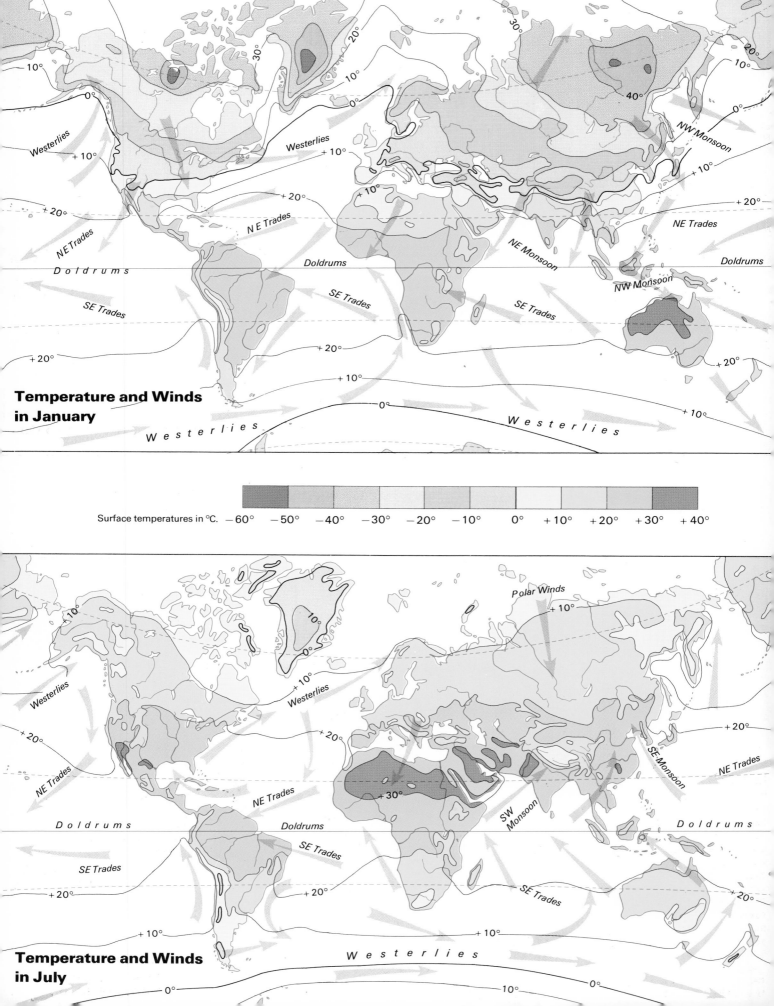

Temperature and Winds in January

Surface temperatures in °C.   −60°   −50°   −40°   −30°   −20°   −10°   0°   +10°   +20°   +30°   +40°

Temperature and Winds in July

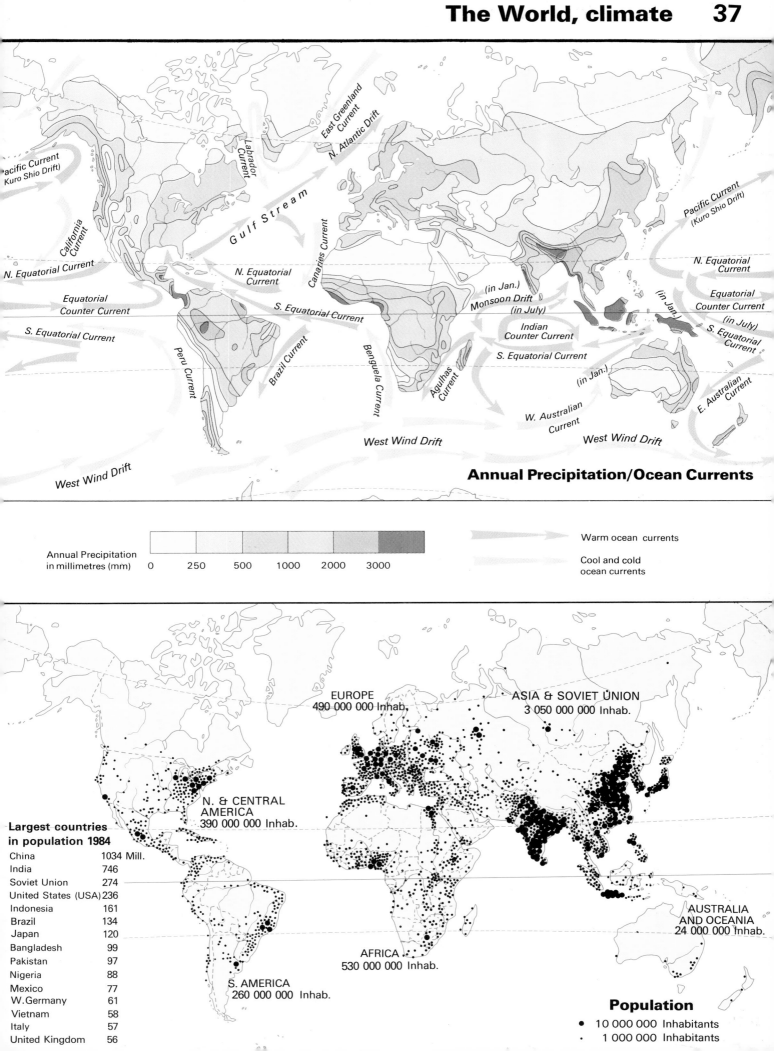

Annual Precipitation/Ocean Currents

Pacific Current
(Kuro Shio Drift)

California Current

N. Equatorial Current

Equatorial Counter Current

S. Equatorial Current

Peru Current

Brazil Current

Labrador Current

East Greenland Current

N. Atlantic Drift

Gulf Stream

N. Equatorial Current

S. Equatorial Current

Canaries Current

Benguela Current

Agulhas Current

Monsoon Drift (in Jan.) (in July)

Indian Counter Current

S. Equatorial Current

W. Australian Current

West Wind Drift

(in Jan.)

(in Jan.)

Pacific Current (Kuro Shio Drift)

N. Equatorial Current

Equatorial Counter Current

(in July) S. Equatorial Current

E. Australian Current

West Wind Drift

West Wind Drift

West Wind Drift

Annual Precipitation
in millimetres (mm)

0   250   500   1000   2000   3000

Warm ocean currents

Cool and cold ocean currents

EUROPE
490 000 000 Inhab.

ASIA & SOVIET UNION
3 050 000 000 Inhab.

N. & CENTRAL AMERICA
390 000 000 Inhab.

AFRICA
530 000 000 Inhab.

S. AMERICA
260 000 000 Inhab.

AUSTRALIA AND OCEANIA
24 000 000 Inhab.

**Largest countries
in population 1984**

China	1034 Mill.
India	746
Soviet Union	274
United States (USA)	236
Indonesia	161
Brazil	134
Japan	120
Bangladesh	99
Pakistan	97
Nigeria	88
Mexico	77
W. Germany	61
Vietnam	58
Italy	57
United Kingdom	56

Population

● 10 000 000 Inhabitants

· 1 000 000 Inhabitants

(A) 150° (A) 180° (B) 150° (C) 120° (D) 90° (E) 60° (F) 30° (G)

① 60°

Kamchatka

Bering Sea

Aleutian Islands

Victoria Island

Baffin Bay

Greenland

Iceland

Arctic Circle

Baffin Island

Bering Strait

Alaska

Mackenzie River

Rocky Mountains

Hudson Bay

Labrador

② NORTH AMERICA

Missouri River

Newfoundland

British Isles

Lon

Chicago

New York

Los Angeles

Mississippi R.

30°

PACIFIC

Tropic of Cancer (23½° N)

Hawaiian Islands

West Indies

Atla

③ OCEAN

Caribbean Sea

ATLANTIC

S

P o l y n e s i a

Central America

0° Equator

River Amazon

OCEAN

④ SOUTH AMERICA

Andes

Tropic of Capricorn (23½ °S)

Rio de Janeiro

30°

Buenos Aires

New Zealand

⑤

■ Million city   International boundary

Pack & drift ice

Cape Horn

Druke Passage

(A) 180° 150° 120° 60° (D) 90° (E) 60° (F) 30° (G)

Glacier, ice cap

Tundra

Coniferous forest

Rain fores

Scale 1:100 000 000
at the Equator

0°0 400 800 km
30°
60° 200 600 1000 km

ARCTIC OCEAN

Spitsbergen

Novaya Zemlya

Barents Sea

North Cape

Norwegian Sea

Ob

Ural Mountains

River Volga

River Ob

S River Yeniset

River Lena

Arctic Circle

Alaska

Bering Strait

S i b e r i a

Aleutian Islands

Bering Sea

Sea of Okhotsk

Kamchatka

River Amur

Manchuria

Moscow

Scandinavia

E U R O P E

Caucasus

Black Sea

Caspian Sea

Altai

A S I A

Gobi

Peking

Seoul

Japan

Tokyo

PACIFIC

Mediterranean Sea

River Euphrates

Tien Shan

Kunlun Shan

Tibet

Himalayas

Hwang Ho

Shanghai

Yangtze Kiang

OCEAN

30°

Cairo

River Nile

Red Sea

Rub al Khali

River Indus

River Ganges

Calcutta

River Mekong

Tropic of Cancer (23½°N)

ara

AFRICA

Bombay

Arabian Sea

Sri Lanka

South China Sea

Philippines

M i c r o n e s i a

M e l a n e s i a

Equator

0°

River Zaire

River Congo

I N D I A N

Sunda Islands

New Guinea

River Zambezi

Madagascar

O C E A N

Coral Sea

4

Kalahari Desert

Tropic of Capricorn (23½°S)

AUSTRALIA

Cape of Good Hope

Darling River

30°

Tasman Sea

Tasmania

New Zealand

5

S O U T H E R N   O C E A N

Cultivated land	Savanna	Steppe	Desert

Ⓐ 150° Ⓑ 180° Ⓒ 150° Ⓓ 120° Ⓔ 90° Ⓕ 60° Ⓖ 30° Ⓗ

② • Verkhoyansk

SOVIET UNION (USSR)

Kolyma

• Magadan 60°

Anadyr •

Bering Str.

Kamchatka

Bering Sea

Aleutian Is. (USA)

Wrangel I.

Beaufort Sea

Queen Elizabeth Islands

Banks I.

Melville Island

Sverdrup Is.

Devon I.

Ellesmere Island

Parry Is.

Greenland
(Denmark)

Jan Mayen
(Norw.)

Baffin Bay

Baffin Island

Victoria Island

Hudson Bay

Labrador

Denmark Strait

Godthåb •

Reykjavik • **ICELAND**

Faeroes

③ Arctic Circle

Alaska
(USA)

Anchorage •

Dawson •

Gulf of Alaska

Yukon

Mackenzie

Rocky Mountains

C A N A D A

Edmonton •

Vancouver •

Seattle •

Winnipeg •

Newfoundland

St. John's •

UNITED KINGDOM
Glasgow
REP. OF IRELAND
Dublin
Lon

Montreal •
Ottawa •
Quebec •
Toronto •
Halifax •

40°

Minneapolis •

UNITED

Salt Lake City •

Chicago •
Detroit •
Boston •
New York •

FRAN

Madrid •

San Francisco •

Denver •

St. Louis •

Philadelphia •
Washington

PORTUGAL
Lisbon
SP

④ **STATES**

Los Angeles •

Dallas •

Mississippi

Bermuda (UK)

Azores (Port.)

Ra

Casablanca •

Houston •

New Orleans •

MOROCCO

Hawaii
(USA)

Tropic of Cancer

Monterrey •

Miami •

G. of Mexico

Habana

THE BAHAMAS

Canary Islands (Sp.)

A

Honolulu 20°

MEXICO

Guadalajara •

Mexico •

Belize

CUBA

HAITI
DOMINICAN REP.

Puerto Rico (U.S.A.)
Santo Domingo

CAPE VERDE ISLANDS

MAURITANIA

SENEGAL
Dakar
Bama

GUATEMALA
Guatemala •

HONDURAS

JAMAICA

Caribbean Sea

BARBADOS

THE GAMBIA
GUINEA-BISSAU
Conakry
GUINEA
UP

EL SALVADOR
NICARAGUA

Managua •
San Jose •

Panama •
Caracas •

GRENADA
TRINIDAD & TOBAGO

SIERRA LEONE
Monrovia
VOL

⑤ **P o l y n e s i a**

COSTA RICA

PANAMA

Medellin •

VENEZUELA
Bogota •

GUYANA
George town
SURINAM
French Guiana

LIBERIA
IVORY COAST
dia
At

COLOMBIA

Equator

Phoenix Is.
(UK/USA)

Galapagos Islands
(Ecuador)

ECUADOR
Quito •

Andes

Amazon

Manaus •

Belém •

Ascension I.
(UK)

Marquesas Is.
(Fr.)

PERU
Lima •

B R A Z I L

Recife •

⑥ **WESTERN SAMOA**
Apia •

Tuamotu Is.
(Fr.)

La Paz •

Brasilia •

Salvador •

St Helena
(UK)

Tahiti

BOLIVIA

Belo Horizonte •

Suva •
FIJI

Sucre •

São Paolo •
Rio de Janeiro •

20° **TONGA**

Cook Is.
(New Zealand)

Pitcairn I.
(UK)

Tropic of Capricorn

PARAGUAY
Asuncion •

O C E A N

Kermadec Is.
(NZ)

Easter I.
(Chile)

Valparaiso •

Rosario •

URUGUAY
Montevideo •

Tristan da Cunha
(UK)

⑦ Santiago •

ARGENTINA

Buenos Aires •

Auckland •

Andes

CHILE

NEW ZEALAND
40° • Wellington

Chatham Is.
(NZ)

Christchurch •

Str. of Magellan

Falkland Islands (UK)

South Georgia (UK)

Bounty I.
(NZ)
Antipodes

Cape Horn

Drake Passage

South Orkney Islands (UK)

South Sandwich Islands (UK)

⑧

South Shetland Islands (UK)

W e d d e l l Sea

■ Recife   Places with over 1 000 000 inh.

• Manaus   Places with under 1 000 000 inh.

● ■ Symbols for capitals (red)

Antarctic Circle

A

60°

⑨ Ⓑ 180° Ⓒ 150° Ⓓ 120° W. Ⓔ 90° Ⓕ 60° Ⓖ 30° Ⓗ

ORIGINS OF THE EARTH

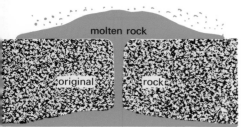

Igneous rocks are formed by the cooling of molten rock; they are called 'extrusive' when forced to the surface or thrown above it.

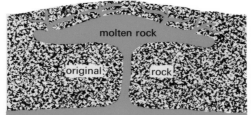

Molten rock not reaching the surface is called 'intrusive'. It cools as solid masses and plugs.

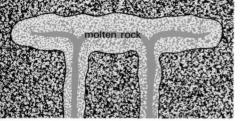

Metamorphic rocks are formed when the original rocks are subjected to intense heat and pressure.

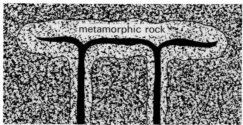

The heat and pressure from molten rock has altered and hardened the surrounding rock and cooled to form metamorphic rock,

The arrows show particles being carried by rivers and rainwater to the sea floor.

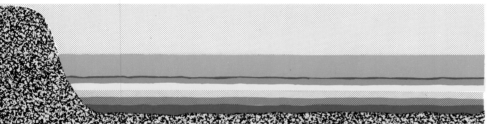

Rainwater and rivers running from the land spread layers of fine soil and silt over the sea floor. Remains of animal and sea plants may also be deposited. From these, sedimentary rocks are formed by the weight of the uppermost layers.

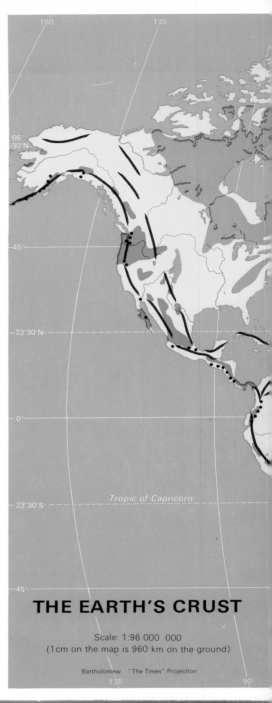

THE EARTH'S CRUST

Scale: 1:96 000 000
(1 cm on the map is 960 km on the ground)

Bartholomew "The Times" Projection

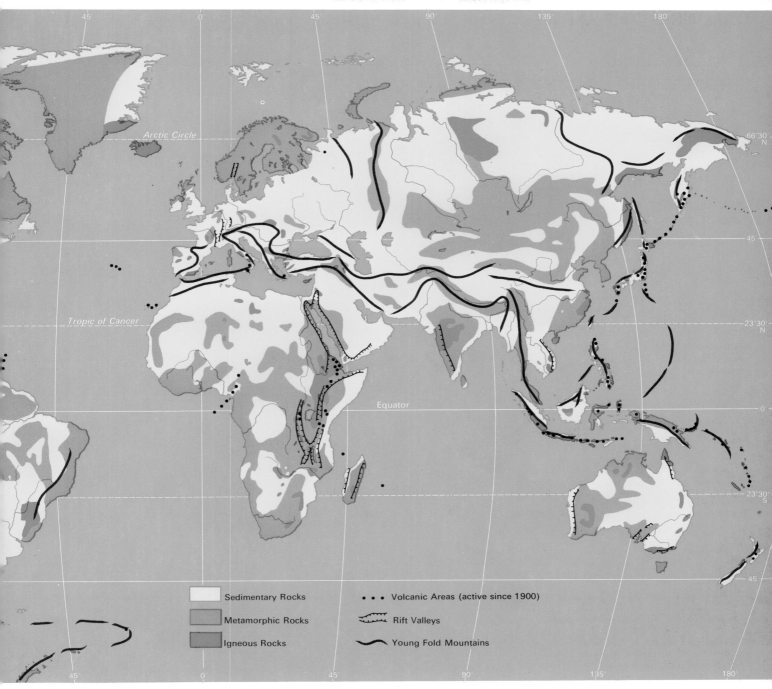

Sedimentary Rocks

Metamorphic Rocks

Igneous Rocks

••• Volcanic Areas (active since 1900)

Rift Valleys

Young Fold Mountains

The origin of the Solar System is not clear. Some scientists believe that 3000 million years ago the Sun and a greater star revolved round each other. At some instant the greater star exploded, distributing most of its material to another part of the galaxy, leaving behind a disc of gas and other matter which remained attracted by, and revolving round, the Sun. This soon gathered into four or five masses which later split into unequal parts, the largest becoming the planets of Saturn, Uranus, Jupiter, Neptune, Earth, Mercury, Venus, Mars and Pluto.

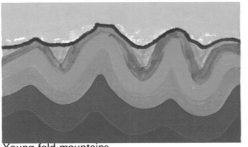

Young fold mountains.

Glaciated U-shaped valley.

Since the Earth was created there have been many changes in its outer appearance and such features as fold mountains, rift valleys and U-shaped valleys have been formed.

The instability of the Earth's crust is evident from volcanoes and earthquakes. Underneath the thin layers of sedimentary rock on the earth's surface are much thicker layers of igneous and metamorphic rock.

Rift valley.

Volcano.

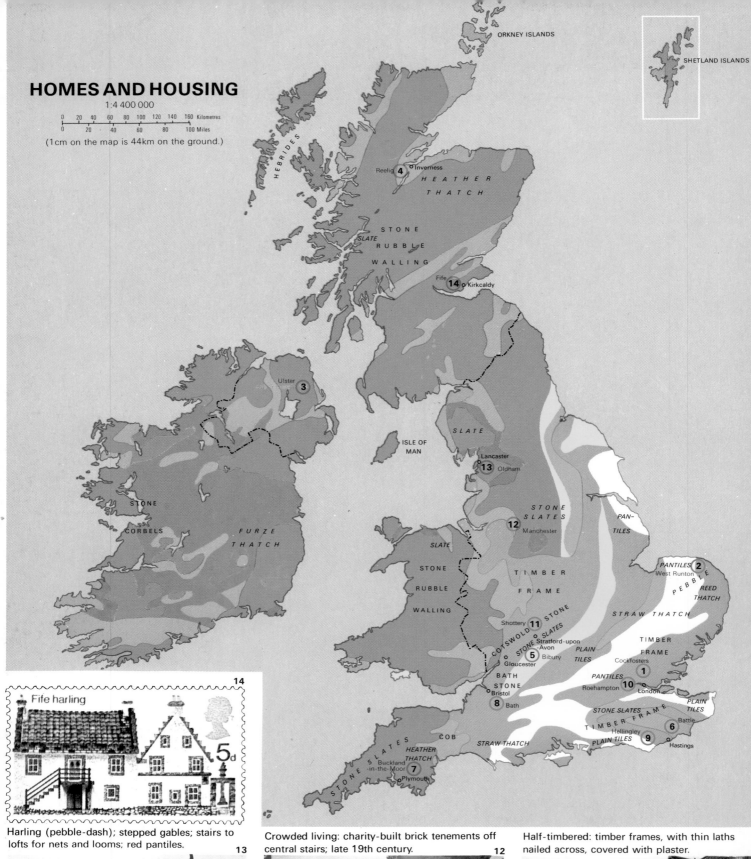

HOMES AND HOUSING
1:4 400 000

0 20 40 60 80 100 120 140 160 Kilometres
0 20 40 60 80 100 Miles

(1cm on the map is 44km on the ground.)

ORKNEY ISLANDS

SHETLAND ISLANDS

HEBRIDES

Reelig ○ Inverness
4
HEATHER THATCH

STONE RUBBLE WALLING
SLATE

Fife **14** ○ Kirkcaldy

Ulster
3

ISLE OF MAN

SLATE

Lancaster
13 ○ Oldham

STONE SLATES

12 Manchester

PAN-TILES

PANTILES **2**
West Runton

STONE CORBELS

FURZE THATCH

SLATE

STONE RUBBLE WALLING

TIMBER FRAME

PEBBLE REED THATCH

STRAW THATCH

Shottery **11** STONE SLATES
COTSWOLD STONE
Stratford-upon-Avon
5 Bibury
○ Gloucester

PLAIN TILES

TIMBER FRAME
Cockfosters
1

PANTILES
Roehampton **10**
London

BATH STONE
8 Bath
○ Bristol

STONE SLATES
TIMBER FRAME
Hellingley **9** **6** Battle
PLAIN TILES
Hastings

PLAIN TILES

COB

STRAW THATCH

STONE SLATES
HEATHER THATCH
Buckland-in-the-Moor
7
○ Plymouth

14
Fife harling
5d

Harling (pebble-dash); stepped gables; stairs to
lofts for nets and looms; red pantiles.

13

Crowding into factory towns led to building of
dreary industrial 'rows'.

Crowded living: charity-built brick tenements off
central stairs; late 19th century. **12**

Half-timbered: timber frames, with thin laths
nailed across, covered with plaster. **1**

44

Suburbs: patterned lay-out; 'little boxes , and they all look just the same'. **1**

East Anglia: durable flint cobble houses, with red clay tiled roofs. **2**

Ulster thatch

Cottage built by country folk from local material: cob (clay and straw) and thatch **3**

VERY OLD, HARD ROCKS granites; slates.

Very ancient rocks in the Scottish Highlands.
Granites originally from Aberdeen (grey); Peterhead (pink); and
Dalbeattie; but now all imported.
Slates split into thin roofing slabs, especially in Wales.
Hard old rocks (sandstone and limestones): Pennines, Wales, Southern
Uplands.
Millstone Grit(coarse sandstone),a fine building stone in Pennines.
These rocks are often used in their rough state (because difficult to
shape, carve or decorate) giving plain simple buildings.
Strong walls and small windows occur where strong winds are
common (eg. in mountains or near coasts).

Typical stone-built Scottish country cottage with dormer windows **4**

SOFTER SANDSTONES

Old Red Sandstones in eastern Scotland, and New Red Sandstones
(eg. in Cheshire).
These beautiful building stones crumble badly, since damp works into
them; frost makes the moisture expand, cracking and splitting the stone.
Many sandstones are too brittle or soft for building.

SOFTER LIMESTONES

Especially in the Cotswolds, but along the limestone ridge.
A nearly perfect building stone: easy to shape and carve; lovely
creamy-yellow. Early used, since found where few forests grew.
Thin slabs used as 'slates'. Unfortunately, attacked and worn away by
acids in the air.

Cotswold limestone; roofing often thin limestone 'slates'. **5**

SOFT CHALK and HARD FLINTS

Kilns burn limestone or chalk to form lime. Mixed with sand, straw
or cowhair, lime gives plaster to weatherproof clay or brick houses.
Cement, from lime, mixed with sand and gravel and with steel
re-inforcement, gives ferro-concrete for many modern buildings. Chalk, too
soft for building, contains lumps of flint used for building in East Anglia.

WOOD,STRAW, CLAYS and BRICK EARTHS

Forests of oak and elm once covered the clay areas, giving strong,
long-lasting timber, for centuries the main housebuilding material
until the forests were destroyed by farmers, charcoal-burners and
shipbuilders.
Thatch came from reeds, and stiff wheat straw.
In the English Midlands, thin wooden strips (laths) nailed across the
large oak or elm upright beams were covered with clay mixed with
straw, and a coating of plaster acted as weatherproofing.
In the river valleys and clay plains, kilns produced bricks and tiles
from brick-earths; shale from coal tips ('bings' in Scotland) was
also used.

Shingled (weather-boarded) houses; black and white half-timbered house in background. **6**

Devonshire cottage, with solid stone walls and thatching. **7**

Attractive modern 'high rises'; problems occur where there is no safe play area. **10**

Brick-built house with hanging tiles. **9**

Royal Crescent: elegant Georgian houses in a planned lay-out; late 18th century. **8**

CITIES AND TOWNS

Some towns began as Roman centres ("chester", "cester", "caster"). With growing trade, medieval towns developed beside a castle, cathedral or monastery with an easily defended site (Stirling Castle rock, river loops round Durham and Shrewsbury). Rivers offered drinking water, and towns arose on fords (Bedford), in gaps (Lincoln), at bridge-points (Gloucester) and as 'central places' (market towns) in fertile plains (York). Coastal towns include fishing ports (Aberdeen, Grimsby), naval stations (Portsmouth), ocean ports (London, Liverpool) and seaside resorts (Brighton, Blackpool). With the Industrial Revolution, towns burst out of their bounds; those on coalfields expanded, with industries often along rivers or canals. Improved transport created "commuting" from suburbs and dormitory towns; the old town centres became the business and shopping districts, with traffic congestion, pollution and slums. Recently, government planning created New Towns, to mop up 'overspill', and give better living and scope for new industries.

Westminster, London - the heart of Britain, with the Abbey and Houses of Parliament.

Edinburgh - a capital; facing its port, Leith, from the Castle rock which dominates routeways.

Newcastle's bridges: Romans, Normans and the *Flying Scotsman* crossed the Tyne here.

Richmond, Yorkshire, whose Norman keep dominates Swaledale.

York - Roman and Anglo-Saxon capital, with Minster and medieval walls and streets.

Cumbernauld, a New Town, won an international award for its planned design.

Norwich - ruled from Old Guildhall and new Town Hall in the market square.

Preston - a mill town's jumble of chimney stacks and workers' red-brick 'rows'.

Oxford, an ancient University town, where cars are made.

Liverpool - major port of north-west England: landing stage, part of docks and Liver buildings.

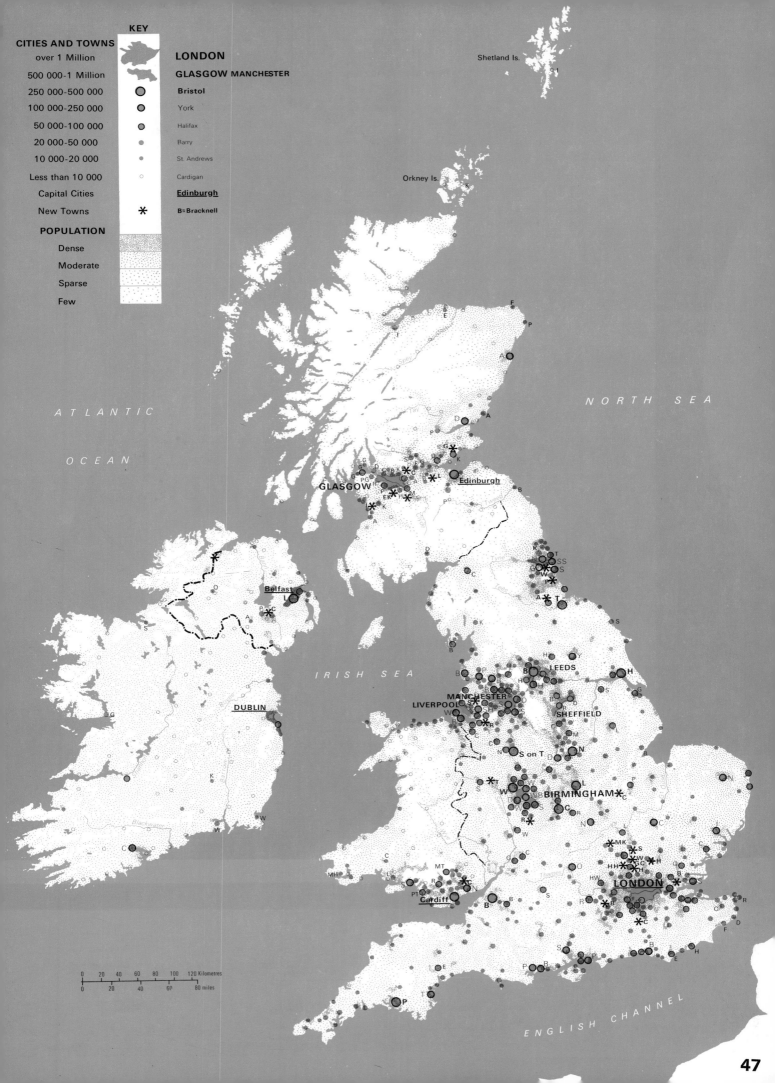

ATLANTIC

OCEAN

NORTH SEA

Shetland Is.

Orkney Is.

GLASGOW <u>Edinburgh</u>

IRISH SEA

Belfast

DUBLIN

LIVERPOOL MANCHESTER

LEEDS

SHEFFIELD

BIRMINGHAM

Cardiff

LONDON

ENGLISH CHANNEL

0   20   40   60   80   100 120 Kilometres
0   20   40   60   80 miles

47

Fawley Refinery, Southampton Water; oil tanker being manoeuvred by tugs

Before the days of steam, machinery was driven by water-wheels.

Bevercotes: a modern coal-mine, with a diesel loco pulling coal trucks.

Finnart, Loch Long, B.P. terminal for pipeline to Grangemouth. Super tanker needs deep water.

Nineteenth century paddle-steamer.

The Barton Aqueduct, swingbridge and oil depot on the Manchester Ship Canal.

B.P. drilling rig "Sea Quest", launched at Belfast, exploring North Sea for oil and natural gas.

Coal pit   Oil field   Reservoir, dam, power station

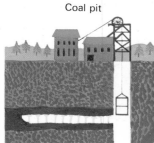

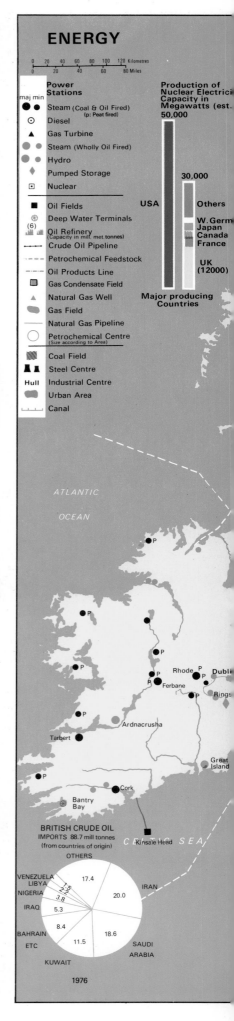

ENERGY

0 20 40 60 80 100 120 Kilometres
0   20   40   60   80 Miles

Power Stations

maj min

● ●   Steam (Coal & Oil Fired)
        (p: Peat fired)
⊙   Diesel
▲   Gas Turbine
●   Steam (Wholly Oil Fired)
●   Hydro
◆   Pumped Storage
⊡   Nuclear

■   Oil Fields
⊛   Deep Water Terminals
(6)   Oil Refinery
     (Capacity in mill. met. tonnes)
╀   Crude Oil Pipeline
- - -   Petrochemical Feedstock
-·-·-   Oil Products Line
▢   Gas Condensate Field
▲   Natural Gas Well
     Gas Field
──   Natural Gas Pipeline
○   Petrochemical Centre
     (Size according to Area)
▨   Coal Field
▮▮   Steel Centre
Hull   Industrial Centre
     Urban Area
└┴┴┘   Canal

Production of Nuclear Electricity Capacity in Megawatts (est.

50,000

USA

30,000

Others

W. Germany
Japan
Canada
France

UK
(12000)

Major producing Countries

ATLANTIC

OCEAN

P

P

P

P

Rhode   P   Dubli
P
P   Ferbane   Rings
P

P

Ardnacrusha

Tarbert

Great Island

P

Cork

Bantry Bay

C   SEA

Kinsale Head

BRITISH CRUDE OIL
IMPORTS 88.7 mill tonnes
(from countries of origin)

OTHERS

VENEZUELA
LIBYA   1.5
   2.2
NIGERIA   3.8
IRAQ   5.3

17.4

20.0

IRAN

BAHRAIN   8.4
ETC

18.6

11.5

SAUDI ARABIA

KUWAIT

1976

HEAT LIGHT AND POWER

The map shows the following labelled locations:

Magnus, Thistle, Dunlin, Murchison, Cormorant, Statfjord, Brent, Heather, Hutton, Ninian, Sullom Voe, Lerwick, Frigg, Beryl, Flotta, Kirkwall, Dounreay, Beatrice, Claymore, Piper, Maureen, Forties, Peterhead, Montrose, Lomond, Cod, Fasnakyle, Foyers, Aberdeen, Ekofisk, Errochty, Rannoch, Clunie, Cruachan, Lochay, Dundee, Auk, Argyll, Sloy, Longannet, Methil, Finnart, Kincardine, Grangemouth (9), Yoker, Glasgow, Cockenzie, Inverkip, Braehead, Edinburgh, Hunterston, Clyde's Mill, Dalmarnock, Blyth, Stella, Chapel-cross, Newcastle, Tongland, Hartlepool, Teesside, fast (1.5), Calder Hall, Billingham (5), Middlesbrough, Kendal, Teesport (6), Lockton, Heysham, Eggborough, Skelton Grange, Drax, West Sole, Leeds, Hull, Manchester, Ferrybridge, Thorpe Marsh, Lindsey (7), Killingholme (4.5), Viking, Liverpool, West Burton, Cottam, Wylfa, Ellesmere Port (1.2), Fiddler's Ferry, Sheffield, High Marnham, Indefatigable, Ffestiniog, Stanlow (10.5), Nottingham, Staythorpe, Leman Bank, Trawsfynydd, Willington, The Wash, Hewett, Rugeley, Ratcliffe, Ironbridge, Drakelow, Castle Donington, Birmingham, Hams Hall, Sizewell, Milford Haven (3), (6.3), Carmarthen Bay, Berkeley, Shell Haven (10), Bradwell, Llandarcy (8), Uskmouth, Oldbury-on-Severn, West Thurrock, Coryton (7), Isle of Grain (10), (5.1), Swansea, Cardiff, Didcot, London, Tilbury, Kingsnorth, Aberthaw, Avonmouth, Portishead, Bristol, Bankside, Northfleet, Belvedere, Richborough, Hinkley Point, Downton, Fawley (16.5), Ashford, Dungeness, Marchwood, Winfrith

NORTH SEA, IRISH SEA, ENGLISH CHANNEL, Moray Firth, Firth of Clyde

John Bartholomew & Son Ltd

Wylfa nuclear power station: twin reactor building in front of turbine hall; coastal location.

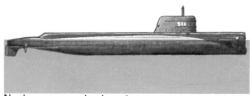

Nuclear-powered submarine

Blaenau-Festiniog pump-storage hydro-electric station. At night, electricity generated pumps water back to reservoir for re-use.

Longannet thermal station: chimney (smoke suppressors;) pylons; pier; reclamation area. Background; Kincardine bridge station.

Longannet: the 8.8 km-long conveyor belt (right) serving 4 mines nears surface. There is also a 'merry-go-round' railway.

OUR WORKSHOPS

The early Industrial Revolution saw the change from craftsmen using simple tools at home and small workshops, to power-driven machinery in factories. Swift streams turned water-wheels to drive machines invented for textile-making; later, with steam power, works arose lower down on coalfields. Today, the electricity grid allows factories to occupy any site with good labour supplies and transport; the Government helps firms to open works in Development Areas with high unemployment and old, dying industries. Britain was once the 'workshop and carrier of the world'; even today, with fierce competition from newer manufacturing countries, Unilever, ICI & BP are among the world's giant concerns.

Map 1. Iron ore, coal and limestone being heavy raw materials, blast furnaces and steelwork developed on coalfields (Sheffield); ore-fields (Scunthorpe) or the coast (Middlesbrough). Many centres (Sheffield, S. Wales, Lanarkshire) had all the raw materials nearby. Huge integrated, automated plants smelt ore, convert pig iron to steel, and roll this into sheets.

Map 2. Motor vehicle centres are scattered, since cars can leave on large transporters, or be driven out. Mass production became possible with the conveyor belt.

Map 3. Separate factories also make car bodies, engines and spare parts, later assembled together.

Map 4. Shipbuilding yards grew on tidal estuaries; overseas competition has caused many to close, and others to merge. Heavy industry emerged near steel-works.

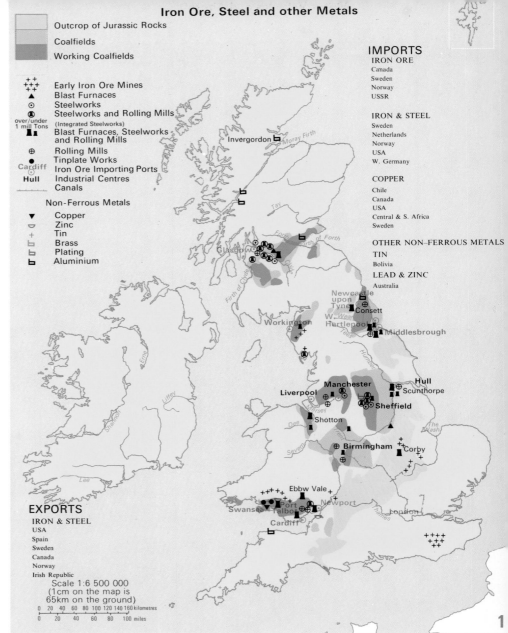

Iron Ore, Steel and other Metals

Outcrop of Jurassic Rocks
Coalfields
Working Coalfields

+ + + Early Iron Ore Mines
▲ Blast Furnaces
⊙ Steelworks
⊛ Steelworks and Rolling Mills
over/under 1 mill Tons (Integrated Steelworks)
Blast Furnaces, Steelworks and Rolling Mills
⊕ Rolling Mills
⊕ Tinplate Works
Cardiff Iron Ore Importing Ports
Hull Industrial Centres
Canals

Non-Ferrous Metals
▼ Copper
▽ Zinc
+ Tin
 b Brass
b Plating
b Aluminium

IMPORTS
IRON ORE
Canada
Sweden
Norway
USSR

IRON & STEEL
Sweden
Netherlands
Norway
USA
W. Germany

COPPER
Chile
Canada
USA
Central & S. Africa
Sweden

OTHER NON-FERROUS METALS
TIN
Bolivia
LEAD & ZINC
Australia

EXPORTS
IRON & STEEL
USA
Spain
Sweden
Canada
Norway
Irish Republic

Scale 1:6 500 000
(1cm on the map is 65km on the ground)

0 20 40 60 80 100 120 140 160 kilometres
0 20 40 60 80 100 miles

1

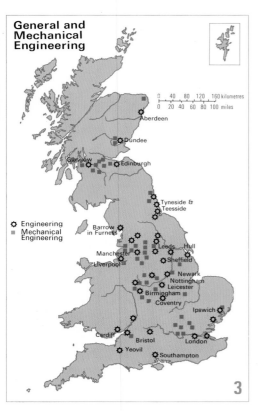

General and Mechanical Engineering

⚙ Engineering
■ Mechanical Engineering

Aberdeen
Dundee
Glasgow
Edinburgh
Tyneside & Teesside
Barrow in Furness
Manchester
Liverpool
Leeds
Hull
Sheffield
Newark
Nottingham
Leicester
Birmingham
Coventry
Ipswich
Cardiff
Bristol
Yeovil
London
Southampton

3

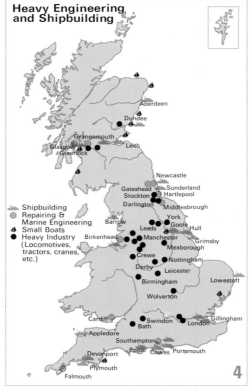

Heavy Engineering and Shipbuilding

🛠 Shipbuilding
◉ Repairing & Marine Engineering
⛵ Small Boats
● Heavy Industry (Locomotives, tractors, cranes, etc.)

Aberdeen
Dundee
Grangemouth
Leith
Glasgow
Greenock
Newcastle
Gateshead
Sunderland
Stockton
Hartlepool
Darlington
Middlesbrough
York
Barrow
Goole
Hull
Birkenhead
Leeds
Manchester
Grimsby
Mexborough
Crewe
Nottingham
Derby
Leicester
Birmingham
Lowestoft
Wolverton
Cardiff
Swindon
Bath
London
Gillingham
Appledore
Southampton
Devonport
Poole
Cowes
Portsmouth
Plymouth
Falmouth

4

Light and Electrical Industries

▲ Light & Electrical Engineering

Glasgow
Newcastle
Keighley
Leeds
Liverpool
Manchester
Lincoln
Stafford
Newark
Nottingham
Birmingham
Rugby
Peterborough
Northampton
Cambridge
Cardiff
Bristol
London
Southampton

5

Motor Vehicles and Aircraft
(Rubber, Tyres and related industries)

Legend:
- ▬ Industrial Areas
- 🚗 Motor Cars, Motor Vehicles
- 🚐 Commercial Vehicles
- 🚜 Earth moving Equipment and tractors
- ✈ Aircraft
- ⊢ Aero Engines
- ● Assembly
- ○ Tyres
- ← Car Exports

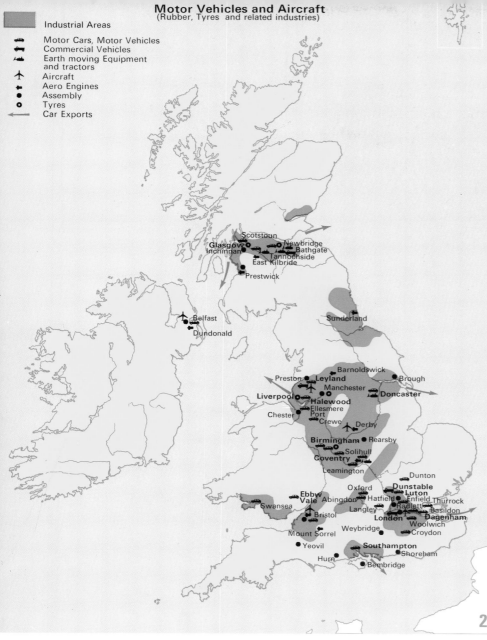

Locations shown on map: Scotstoun, Glasgow, Inchinnan, Newbridge, Bathgate, Tannochside, East Kilbride, Prestwick, Belfast, Dundonald, Sunderland, Barnoldswick, Brough, Preston, Leyland, Manchester, Doncaster, Liverpool, Halewood, Ellesmere Port, Chester, Crewe, Derby, Birmingham, Rearsby, Solihull, Coventry, Leamington, Dunton, Ebbw Vale, Abingdon, Oxford, Hatfield, Dunstable, Luton, Enfield, Thurrock, Langley, Radlett, Basildon, Swansea, Bristol, London, Dagenham, Woolwich, Weybridge, Croydon, Mount Sorrel, Yeovil, Southampton, Shoreham, Hurn, Bembridge

Map 5. Light and electrical industry, including a bewildering variety of products, is common in the suburbs of big towns, along main roads, and in special zones in planned Industrial Estates and New Towns, often in pre-fabricated factories.

Map 6. Bricks (from clay) and cement (from chalk) are made where these materials occur.

Map 7. The salt fields provided raw materials for soap, bleaches, and dyes (later made from coal tar). Petrochemicals from oil refineries at seaports, move cheaply via pipelines (the 'pipeline revolution'.) Man-made fibres and plastics have changed our lives since 1945.

Map 8. Paper-making, using bulky wood, 'esparto' pulp and much water, is found on rivers and near ports. Printing and publishing have long been connected with universities, legal offices and business centres.

Irish Industries

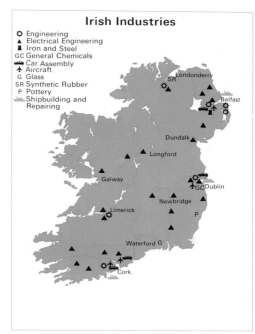

Legend:
- ⬡ Engineering
- ▲ Electrical Engineering
- ◼ Iron and Steel
- GC General Chemicals
- 🚗 Car Assembly
- ✈ Aircraft
- G Glass
- SR Synthetic Rubber
- P Pottery
- ⤳ Shipbuilding and Repairing

Locations: Londonderry, Belfast, Dundalk, Longford, Galway, Dublin, Newbridge, Limerick, Waterford, Cork

Building and Household

- B Bricks
- C Cement
- Sl Slate
- G Granite
- Sa Sandstone
- Ch China
- K Kaolin
- Sa Saw Milling
- T Timber
- F Furniture
- H Hardware
- C Cutlery
- S Sewing Machines
- W Washing Machines, Refrigerators
- T Tools & Implements
- L Linoleum & Linotiles
- G Glass

Locations: Corpach, Aberdeen, Oban, Tayport, Singer, Kirkcaldy, Glasgow, Dunbar, Penicuik, Kilmarnock, Creetown, Newcastle, Hartlepool, Lancaster, Leeds, Hull, Liverpool, Manchester, Sheffield, St. Helens, Stoke, Wolverhampton, Birmingham, Rugby, Peterborough, Great Yarmouth, Worcester, Bedford, Cardiff, Bristol, London, Southampton, St. Austell

6

Chemicals and Plastics

- GC General Chemicals
- S Soap
- D Detergents
- Ph Pharmaceuticals
- Dy Dyestuffs
- ○ Petrochemical Centres
- R Rubber(Imported)
- SR Synthetic Rubber
- CP Chemical Products (Made from Rubber)
- RP Rubber Plastics
- RG Rubber Goods
- NM Nuclear Materials
- F Fertilisers

Locations: Aberdeen, Perth, Dundee, Glasgow, Leith, Grangemouth, Ardrossan, Galashiels, Newcastle, Durham, Billingham, Barnard Castle, Teesside, Middlesbrough, Sellafield, Hull, Selwick, Liverpool, Manchester, Birkenhead, Northwich, Capenhurst, Nottingham, Leicester, Norwich, Birmingham, Ipswich, Harwich, Colchester, Swansea, Pontypool, London, Slough, Hythe

(Area pecked under constn.)

7

Paper, Printing and Publishing

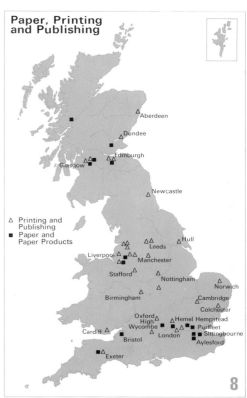

- △ Printing and Publishing
- ◼ Paper and Paper Products

Locations: Aberdeen, Dundee, Edinburgh, Glasgow, Newcastle, Leeds, Hull, Liverpool, Manchester, Stafford, Nottingham, Norwich, Birmingham, Cambridge, Colchester, Oxford, High Wycombe, Hemel Hempstead, Purfleet, Cardiff, London, Sittingbourne, Bristol, Aylesford, Exeter

8

51

BRITISH CLIMATE
Temperature

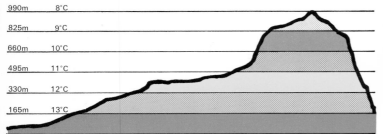

Temperature decreases with altitude by about 1°C per 165m rise. The Sun's rays heat the Earth which in turn heats the atmosphere.

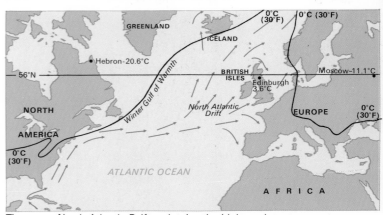

The warm North Atlantic Drift maintains the higher winter temperatures around the coasts of Britain and Western Europe the Winter Gulf of Warmth. Some mean January temperatures are given.

WINTER (January Temperatures)

Very mild		Over 6°C (over 42°Fahr.)
Mild		5-6°C (41-42°Fahr.)
Cool		4-5°C (39-41°Fahr.)
Cold		3-4°C (37.4-39° Fahr.)
Coldest		below 3°C (below 37.4°Fahr.)

SUMMER (July Temperatures)

Warmest		Over 17°C (Over 62.6°Fahr.)
Very warm		16-17°C (61-62.6°Fahr.)
Warm		15-16°C (59-61°Fahr.)
Cool		14-15°.C (57-59°Fahr.)
Coolest		below 14°C (below 57°Fahr.)

South-facing slopes are warmer than those facing north both by being sheltered from cold north winds, and from a greater concentration of the Sun's rays which they receive due to the steeper angle of incidence.

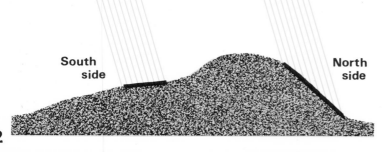

Temperature decreases from the Equator to the Poles since, near the Poles the Sun's rays fall more obliquely on the Earth's surface and have a longer passage through the heat-absorbing atmosphere than the rays nearer the Equator.

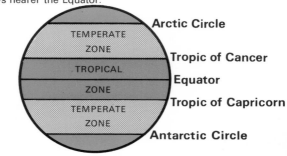

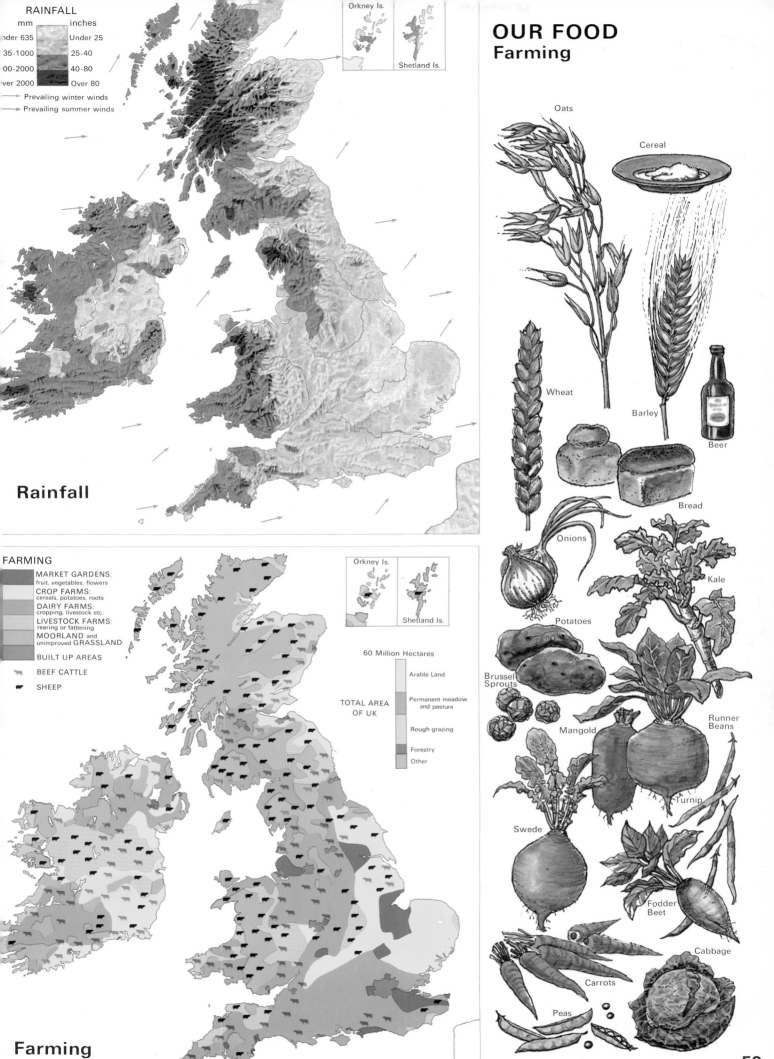

RAINFALL

mm	inches
under 635	Under 25
635-1000	25-40
1000-2000	40-80
over 2000	Over 80

→ Prevailing winter winds
→ Prevailing summer winds

Orkney Is.

Shetland Is.

Rainfall

FARMING

MARKET GARDENS:
fruit, vegetables, flowers

CROP FARMS:
cereals, potatoes, roots

DAIRY FARMS:
cropping, livestock etc.

LIVESTOCK FARMS:
rearing or fattening

MOORLAND and
unimproved GRASSLAND

BUILT UP AREAS

BEEF CATTLE

SHEEP

Orkney Is.

Shetland Is.

60 Million Hectares

Arable Land

Permanent meadow
and pasture

TOTAL AREA
OF UK

Rough grazing

Forestry

Other

Farming

OUR FOOD
Farming

Oats

Cereal

Wheat

Barley

Beer

Bread

Onions

Kale

Potatoes

Brussel
Sprouts

Mangold

Runner
Beans

Turnip

Swede

Fodder
Beet

Cabbage

Carrots

Peas

OUR FOOD
From the land

Aberdeen Angus (beef)

Hereford (beef)

Ayrshire (dairy)

Border Leicester

Wessex Saddleback

Poultry

Dairy produce

Fruit

C	Cider
B	Beer
W	Whisky
F	Flour
B	Biscuits
C	Confectionery
Cho	Chocolate
S	Cane Sugar
Sb	Beet Sugar
Ca	Canning (fruit, vegetables, jam)
Fp	Food processing
Ba	Bacon
P	Poultry
M	Milk processing
Bu	Butter
Ch	Cheese
A	Agricultural engineering
Ac	Agricultural chemicals
F	Fertilisers
S	Salt

Shetland Is.

PIGS 8 million
CATTLE 12 million
SHEEP 27 million

TOTAL LIVESTOCK UK

⊙ Principal livestock markets in U.K.

▢ Population density 500 per Km²

1:6 800 000

0 ——— 160 Kilometres
0 ——— 100 Miles

1cm on the map is 68km on the ground

Blackface sheep seen near stone & slated buildings on moorland.

British Friesian dairy cows grazing on water meadows.

Most British farming is 'mixed', handling both crops and animals, and is possibly the most highly scientific and mechanised in the world. Grain, potatoes and sugar beet all do best on the rich, drier eastern arable plains, with warm, sunny summers - oats can withstand wetter conditions. Market gardening is profitable near big city markets. Berry and orchard fruits, bulbs in 'Little Holland', early flowers from Cornwall and Scilly, hops in Kent and cider apples in Sussex and Hereford, all need special care and plentiful labour.

Sheep are found on mountain slopes, chal[k] and limestone hills, and also cropped land. Dairying is common on rainy western plai[n] and near large populations. Beef cattle, including the world's finest breeds, often e[at] fodder crops, especially barley.
(Look also at map on page 23).

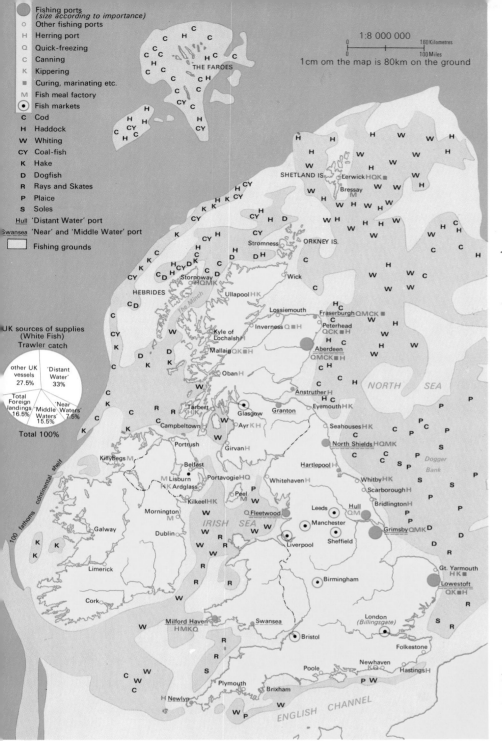

Legend:

- ● Fishing ports (size according to importance)
- ○ Other fishing ports
- H Herring port
- Q Quick-freezing
- C Canning
- K Kippering
- ■ Curing, marinating etc.
- M Fish meal factory
- ⊙ Fish markets
- C Cod
- H Haddock
- W Whiting
- CY Coal-fish
- K Hake
- D Dogfish
- R Rays and Skates
- P Plaice
- S Soles
- Hull 'Distant Water' port
- Swansea 'Near' and 'Middle Water' port
- ▫ Fishing grounds

UK sources of supplies (White Fish) Trawler catch

- other UK vessels 27.5%
- 'Distant Water' 33%
- Total Foreign landings 16.5%
- 'Middle Waters' 15.5%
- 'Near Waters' 7.5%
- Total 100%

THE FAROES

SHETLAND IS. — Lerwick HQK — Bressay M

ORKNEY IS. — Stromness — Wick

NORTH SEA

Dogger Bank

HEBRIDES — Stornoway HQMK — Ullapool HK — Lossiemouth — Inverness Q ■ H — Fraserburgh QMCK ■ — Peterhead QCK ■ — Aberdeen QMCK ■ — Kyle of Lochalsh — Mallaig QK ■ — Oban H — Anstruther H — Eyemouth HK — Seahouses HK — North Shields HQMK — Hartlepool — Whitehaven H — Whitby HK — Scarborough H — Bridlington H — Hull QM — Grimsby QMK D — Gt. Yarmouth HK ■ — Lowestoft QK ■ H

Stornoway HQMK

Tarbert HK — Glasgow — Granton — Campbeltown — Ayr KH — Girvan H — Portrush — Belfast — Portavogie HQ — Peel — Lisburn M — Ardglass NK — Kilkeel HK — Mornington M — Leeds — Manchester — Sheffield — Liverpool — Killybegs M — Dublin — IRISH SEA — Fleetwood — Birmingham — London (Billingsgate) — Galway — Limerick — Cork — Milford Haven HMKQ — Swansea — Bristol — Newhaven KQ — Hastings H — Folkestone — Poole — Plymouth — Brixham — Newlyn H — ENGLISH CHANNEL

The Minch

100 fathoms continental shelf

1:8 000 000
160 Kilometres / 100 Miles
1cm om the map is 80km on the ground

Lower map:

CANADA — LABRADOR — NEWFOUNDLAND — Grand Bank — GREENLAND — SPITSBERGEN — BEAR I. — BARENTS SEA — ICELAND — NORWEGIAN SEA — THE FAROES — ROCKALL — NORTH SEA — NORWAY — NORTH ATLANTIC OCEAN

Cod Red-fish — Cod Haddock Plaice — Cod Haddock Red-fish — Cod Haddock Coal-fish Red-fish — Cod Red-fish Cat-fish — Cod — Haddock Coal-fish — Haddock Skate Ling

Aberdeen — Granton — North Shields — Hull — Fleetwood — Grimsby — Lowestoft — Newlyn

100 fathoms continental shelf

'Distant Water' landings

- Iceland 41%
- Barents Sea 34%
- Norwegian Coast 16%
- Bear Island 7%
- Greenland 1%
- Newfoundland & Labrador 1%

800 Kilometres / 500 Miles

— Trawler routes to 'Distant Water' fishing grounds
--- Trawler routes to Near and Middle Water grounds
▫ Fishing grounds
vvv Winter limit of pack-ice

OUR FOOD
From the sea

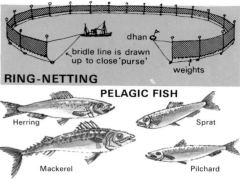

RING-NETTING

bridle line is drawn up to close 'purse' — dhan — weights

PELAGIC FISH

Herring — Sprat — Mackerel — Pilchard

In the mainly Scottish herring fishing, pairs of boats make a ring of net, or pull a trawl near the surface.

TRAWLING

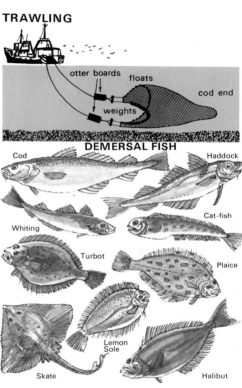

otter boards — floats — cod end — weights

DEMERSAL FISH

Cod — Haddock — Whiting — Cat-fish — Turbot — Plaice — Lemon Sole — Skate — Halibut

Large (freezer) trawlers and factory ships belong to big companies. The smaller, cheaper seine-netters fish nearer to our coasts.

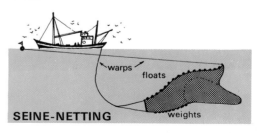

SEINE-NETTING

warps — floats — weights

Lobsters, flown live in tanks to market, and prawns ('scampi') are valuable catches (sometimes more so than herrings in Scotland).

SHELL FISH

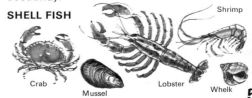

Crab — Mussel — Lobster — Shrimp — Whelk

OUR HOLIDAYS AT HOME

Britain is blessed by beautiful, varied scenery: rocky coves, sandy beaches, gentle downs, grand mountains and lovely old towns; menaced by modern life, they are protected for our leisure activities.

M50 motorway near Ross-on-Wye.

Anglo-French Concorde airliner.

Norfolk Broads: inland waterways with yachts and holiday cabin-cruisers.

Braemar Highland Gathering, near the Queen's castle of Balmoral.

Golden Mile, Blackpool.

Tattoo, Edinburgh Castle; during Festival.

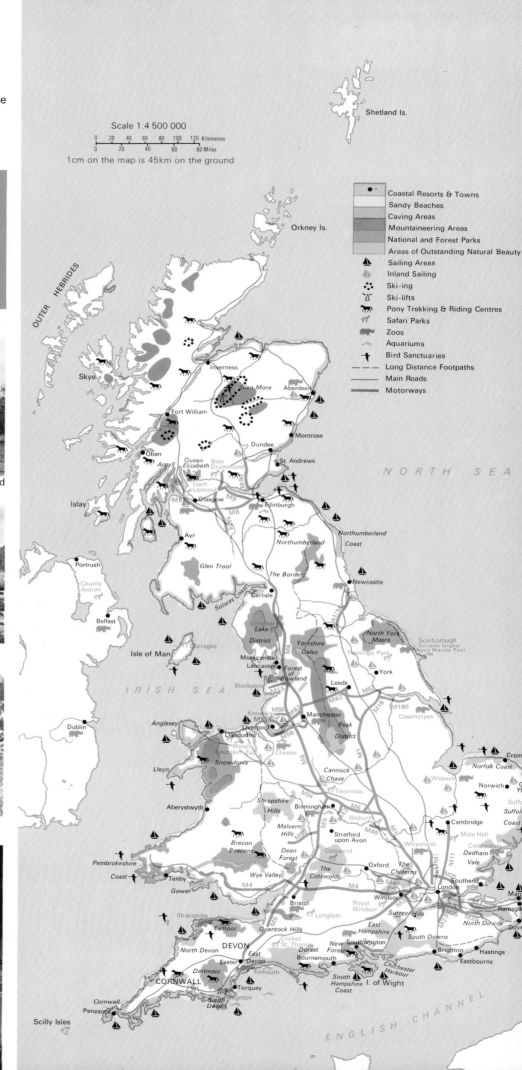

Scale 1:4 500 000

0 20 40 60 80 100 120 Kilometres
0 20 40 60 80 Miles

1cm on the map is 45km on the ground

Legend

- Coastal Resorts & Towns
- Sandy Beaches
- Caving Areas
- Mountaineering Areas
- National and Forest Parks
- Areas of Outstanding Natural Beauty
- Sailing Areas
- Inland Sailing
- Ski-ing
- Ski-lifts
- Pony Trekking & Riding Centres
- Safari Parks
- Zoos
- Aquariums
- Bird Sanctuaries
- Long Distance Footpaths
- Main Roads
- Motorways

Map labels

Shetland Is.
Orkney Is.
OUTER HEBRIDES
Skye
Inverness
Glen More
Aberdeen
Fort William
Oban
Argyll
Queen Elizabeth
Blair Drummond
Dundee
Montrose
St. Andrews
Loch Lomond
Islay
Glasgow
Edinburgh
Ayr
Northumberland
Northumberland Coast
Portrush
County Antrim
Glen Trool
The Border
Newcastle
Carlisle
Solway Coast
Belfast
Lake District
Lowther
Yorkshire Dales
North York Moors
Scarborough Europe's largest Aqua Marine Pool
Flamingo Park
Isle of Man
Curraghs
Morecambe
Lancaster
Forest of Bowland
Leeds
York
NORTH SEA
IRISH SEA
Blackpool
Dublin
Anglesey
Knowsley
Liverpool
Manchester
Peak District
Cleethorpes
Llandudno
Welsh Mountain Zoo
Chester
Snowdonia
Lleyn
Cannock Chase
Cromer
Norfolk Coast
Wisbech
Aberystwyth
Shropshire Hills
Birmingham
Twycross
Norwich
Gt. Yarmouth
Suffolk Coast
Malvern Hills
Stratford upon Avon
Woburn
Cambridge
Mole Hall
Brecon Beacons
Dean Forest
Cotswold
Whipsnade
Dedham Vale
Pembrokeshire Coast
Tenby
Gower
Wye Valley
The Cotswolds
Oxford
The Chilterns
London
Southend
Margate
Bristol
Longleat
Royal Windsor
Windsor
Surrey Hills
North Downs
Ramsgate
Dover
Ilfracombe
Exmoor
Quantock Hills
East Hampshire
South Downs
Hastings
Eastbourne
North Devon
DEVON
East Devon
Cricket St. Thomas
Dorset
New Forest
Southampton
Chichester Harbour
Brighton
Dartmoor
Exeter
Exmouth
South Hampshire Coast
I. of Wight
CORNWALL
Torquay
Paignton
South Devon
Cornwall Coast
Penzance
Scilly Isles
ENGLISH CHANNEL

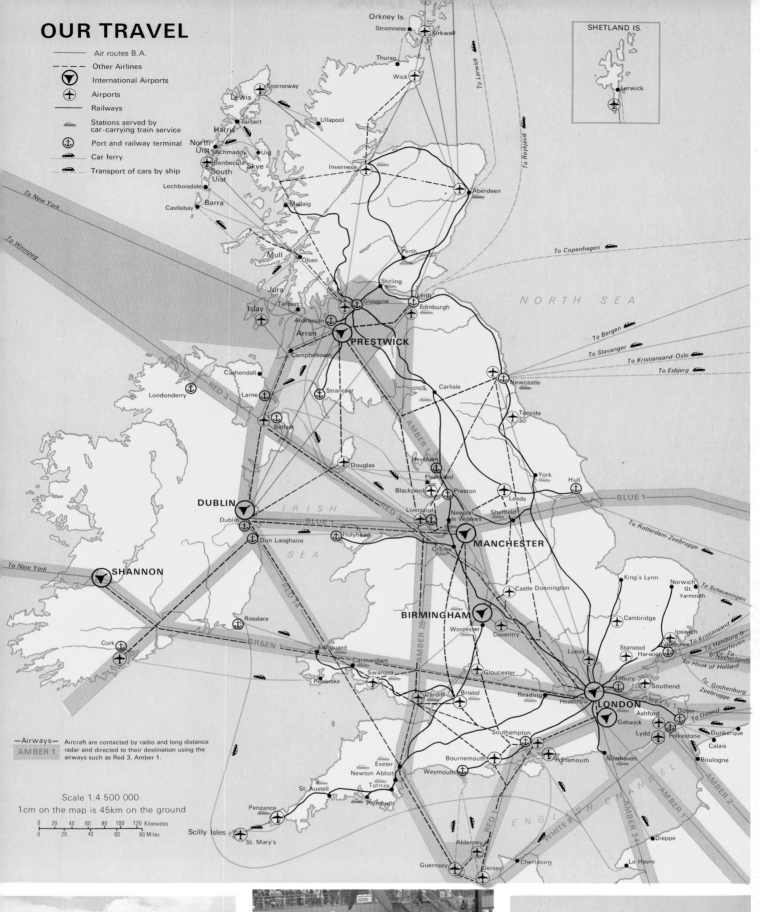

OUR TRAVEL

Air routes B.A.
Other Airlines
International Airports
Airports
Railways
Stations served by car-carrying train service
Port and railway terminal
Car ferry
Transport of cars by ship

—Airways— Aircraft are contacted by radio and long distance
AMBER 1 radar and directed to their destination using the airways such as Red 3, Amber 1.

Scale 1:4 500 000
1cm on the map is 45km on the ground

Q.E. II built (1967) at Brown's, Clydebank.
Q.E. I sank 1972 in Hong Kong harbour.

London's Airports (Heathrow and Gatwick): both very congested.

Hovercraft, a British invention.

57

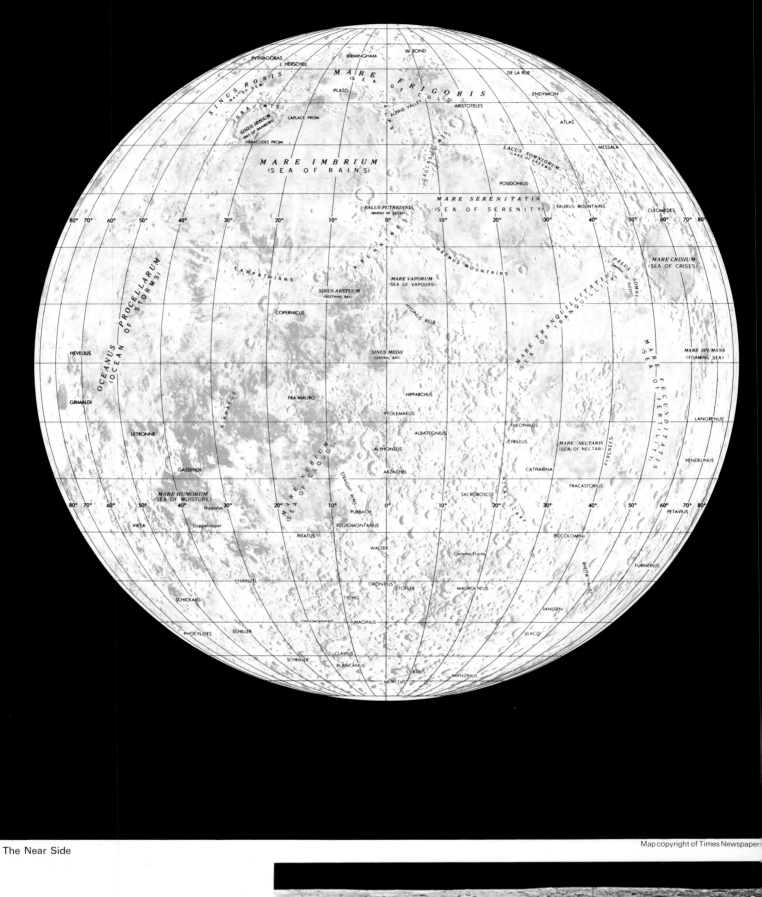

The Near Side

THE MOON

The Surface.

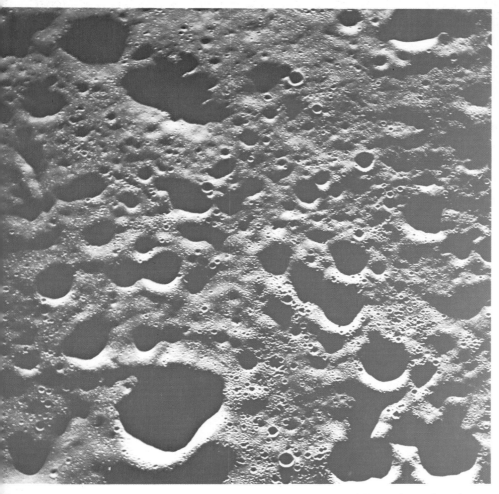

Rocket blast-off.

"That's one small step for a man, one giant leap for mankind", said the first 'Man on the Moon', the Apollo 11 Astronaut Neil Armstrong on July 20; 1969. The Moon, (diameter 3476km) orbits our Earth once every lunar month. The lunar landscape shows broad, flat plains or lunar 'seas', mountain ranges and thousands of craters. Although barren, silent and airless, it is an excellent site for space stations and scientific observatories.

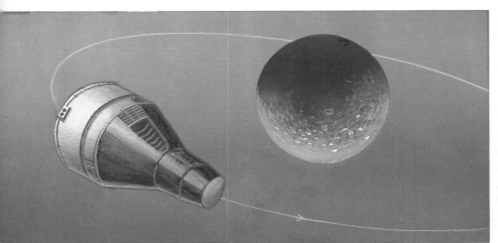

Spacecraft in orbit.

Lunar walk.

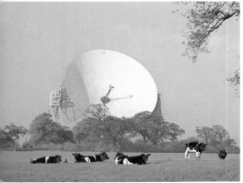

Radio-Telescope, Jodrell Bank.

There are two high and low tides daily, when the Sun and Moon are directly opposite, or at right angles, to one another.

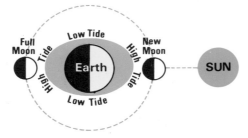

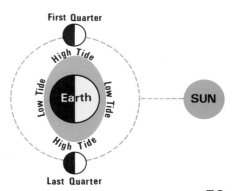

THE UNIVERSE

Man once believed that the world and the universe were the same thing. The Earth was thought to be the centre of the universe and the largest object in it and stars were viewed as points of light on the sky.

Scientists now tell us that Earth is merely a speck in the great vastness of the universe and that stars are distant suns. Billions of stars make up one galaxy and there are millions of galaxies of different shapes. It would take 6000 million years travelling at the speed of light (299 783 km per second) to reach the limit of the observed universe.

Our Solar System

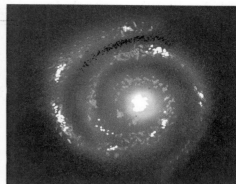

Full view of a spiral galaxy rotating in a sea of dust and gas.

Elliptical galaxy. Shows few signs of cosmic gas and dust.

Spiral galaxy. Note trailing arms and nucleus.

Edge-on view of a spiral galaxy. Nucleus consists of millions of stars. Dark markings are clouds of cosmic dust.

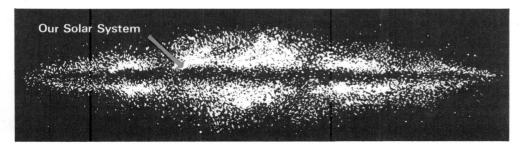

Our Solar System

The ancients saw-as you can see-a broad, faint band of light extending across the heavens. They thought it was a milk-white road for the gods-a Milky Way System the galaxy to which our planet belongs.

61

Pluto

Neptune

Uranus

Saturn

THE SOLAR SYSTEM

The Sun contains over 99.87 of the total mass in our Solar System and completely dominates its nine major planets and thousands of tiny planets called 'asteroids'. Although Jupiter is roughly 1300 times the size of the Earth it is a mere speck by comparison with the Sun.

though Mars may possess some form of life. Mercury and Venus are much too close to the Sun to support any form of life and Neptune and Pluto are much too cold.

The planets are held near the Sun by the pull of gravity and revolve round it in elliptical orbits. The Earth is 150 million km from the Sun and travels at 29.8 km per second, or approximately 107 180 km per hour and completes its orbit in one year. The Earth is the only known planet to have life on it,

The planets shown here are seen from a point in space. Because of the great distance, the Sun looks very small, and the planets themselves are not true to scale

Jupiter

Mars

Earth

Mercury

Venus

On clear nights Mercury, Venus, Mars, Jupiter and Saturn are visible without a telescope, Uranus can just be seen, but Neptune and Pluto can only be seen through a telescope. A planet differs from a star in that it gives out a more steady light and travels across the sky. The position of a planet can be found in a 'timetable' for the planets(an almanack or ephemeris) in the local library.

The Sun, which is a star, is the source of light reflected by the planets.

Planet	Distance from Sun (million km)	Time of Orbit around Sun	
		Years	Days
Mercury	58	0	88
Venus	108	0	225
Earth	150	1	0
Mars	229	1	322
Jupiter	777	11	315
Saturn	1426	29	167
Uranus	2870	84	7
Neptune	4495	164	284
Pluto	5900	248	120

INDEX

How to find a place in the atlas

This index shows you where to find the most important places in the atlas.
It tells you where the place is on the largest scale map that shows it.
The index is written like this:

name   description   page column row
Aberdeen   (city in Scotland) **20**   C   2

1. First find page 20.
2. Now look for the columns that run down the page. find column C.
3. Then look for the rows that run across the page. Find row 2.
4. There is a box where column C crosses row 2. Aberdeen is in this box.
   Point to Aberdeen.

Abbreviations

Arch.	archipelago
bet.	between
Central Afr. Rep.	Central African Republic
E.	East
G.	Gulf
I.	Island
Is.	Islands
N.	North
penin.	peninsula
Rep. of Ireland	Republic of Ireland
Scot.	Scotland
S.	South
U.S.S.R.	Soviet Union
U.S.A.	United States of America
W.	West

A

Aberdeen (city in Scotland) 20 C2
Aberystwyth (town in Wales) 18 B3
Abidjan (capital of Ivory Coast) 27 B4
Acapulco (town in Mexico) 29 J7
Accra (capital of Ghana) 27 B4
Aconcagua (highest peak in the Andes) 31 C7
Addis Ababa (capital of Ethiopia) 27 F4
Adelaide (city in Australia) 33 C6
Aden (town in South Yemen) 27 G3
Aden, Gulf of 27 G3
Adriatic Sea 23 M8
Aegean Sea 23 O9
Afghanistan (Asia) 25 H5
Africa (continent) 39 H3
Ahmadabad (city in India) 41 L4
Alaska (U.S.A.) 29 C2
Alaska, Gulf of 29 D3
Albania (Europe) 23 N8
Alderney (island in the Channel Islands) 18 C5
Aleutian Is. (island chain of Alaska) 29 A3
Alexandria (city in Egypt) 27 E1
Algeria (Africa) 27 B2
Algiers (capital of Algeria) 27 C1
Allen, Bog of (Ireland) 21 B3
Alps, The (mountain range in Europe) 23 L7
Altai (mountain range in Asia) 39 K2
Amazon R. Second longest river in the world, 31 E4 draining the largest area. Flows 6570 km (4080 miles) from the Andes across Peru and Brazil through vast rain forests to the Atlantic Ocean. Navigable to Iquitos for ocean going vessels.
Amman (capital of Jordan) 27 F1
Amsterdam (capital of the Netherlands) 23 K6
Amur R. N. China/U.S.S.R. Formed by joining 25 O3 of Argun and Shilka Rs. Flows 4354 km (2700 miles) to Pacific Ocean. Forms U.S.S.R./China boundary for much of its length.
Anadyr (town in U.S.S.R.) 41 O2
Anatolia (peninsula in W. Asia) 23 P9
Anchorage (town in Alaska) 29 D2
Andaman Islands (India) 25 L7
Andes (mountain range in South America) 31 D6
Andorra (Europe) 23 K8
Anglesey (island in Wales) 19 B3
Angola (Africa) 27 D6
Ankara (capital of Turkey) 23 O9
Antananarivo (capital of Madagascar) 27 G6
Antipodes (island group in the Pacific Ocean) 40 B8
Apia (capital of Western Samoa) 40 C6
Appalachian Mountains (North America) 29 K5
Arabian Sea 25 H7
Arafura Sea 33 C3
Aral Sea 25 G4
Aran Islands (Ireland) 21 B3
Arctic Ocean 34 O
Ardnamurchan Point (most westerly point 20 A2 of Scottish mainland)
Argentina (South America) 31 D6
Arkhangel'sk (town in Soviet Union) 25 F2
Armagh (town in Northern Ireland) 21 C2
Arran (island in Scotland) 20 B3
Ascension I. (island in the Atlantic Ocean) 40 H6
Asia (continent) 39 K2
Asunción (capital of Paraguay) 31 E6
Athens (capital of Greece) 23 O9
Athlone (town in Rep. of Ireland) 21 B3
Atlantic Ocean 38 F3
Atlas Mountains (Africa) 27 B1
Auckland (city in New Zealand) 33 G6
Auckland Is. (group of islands S. of 41 P8 New Zealand)
Australian Alps (mountain range in Australia) 33 D6
Austria (Europe) 23 M7
Aviemore (town in Scotland) 20 C2

Ayr (town in Scotland) 20 B3
Azores (islands in Atlantic Ocean) 40 H4

B

Baffin Bay (gulf between Canada and 38 E1 Greenland)
Baffin I. (Canada) 29 L2
Baghdad (capital of Iraq) 27 G1
Bahamas, The (islands in Atlantic Ocean) 29 L6
Bahrain (islands in Asia) 27 H2
Baku (city in Soviet Union) 25 F4
Balkhash, Lake (Soviet Union) 25 J4
Baltic Sea 23 N5
Bamako (capital of Mali) 27 B3
Bandung (town in Indonesia) 41 M6
Banff (town in Scotland) 20 C2
Bangalore (city in India) 41 L5
Bangkok (capital of Thailand) 25 L7
Bangladesh (Asia) 25 L6
Bangui (capital of Central Afr. Rep.) 27 D4
Banjul (capital of Gambia) 27 A3
Banks I. (Canada) 29 F1
Bann (river in Ireland) 21 C2
Bantry (town in Rep. of Ireland) 21 B4
Bantry Bay (Ireland) 21 B4
Barbados (island in the West Indies) 31 E2
Barcelona (city in Spain) 23 K8
Barents Sea 23 Q2
Barmouth (town in Wales) 18 B3
Bass Strait (channel between Australia 33 D6 and Tasmania)
Bath (city in England) 18 C4
Baykal, Lake (Soviet Union) 25 M3
Beaufort Sea 29 B1
Beira (town in Mozambique) 27 F7
Beirut (capital of Lebanon) 27 F1
Belém (city in Brazil) 40 G6
Belfast (capital of Northern Ireland) 21 D2
Belgium (Europe) 23 K6
Belgrade (capital of Yugoslavia) 23 N8
Belize (Central America) 29 K7
Belmopan (capital of Belize) 29 K7
Belo Horizonte (city in Brazil) 40 G6
Ben Nevis (mountain in Scotland) 20 B2
Bengal, Bay of 25 K7
Benghazi (city in Libya) 27 E1
Benin (Africa) 27 C4
Bergen (city in Norway) 23 K4
Bering Sea 39 N2
Bering Strait (channel between U.S.S.R. 25 V2 and Alaska)
Berlin (largest city in Germany) 23 M6
Bermuda (island group in Atlantic Ocean) 29 M5
Bern (capital of Switzerland) 23 L7
Berwick (town in England) 20 C3
Bhutan (Asia) 25 L6
Birmingham (city in England) 18 C3
Biscay, Bay of 22 H7
Bismarck Arch. (volcanic islands E. of 41 N6 New Guinea)
Bissau (capital of Guinea-Bissau) 27 A3
Black Sea 23 Q8
Blackburn (town in England) 19 C3
Blackpool (town in England) 19 C3
Blue Nile (river in Africa) 27 F3
Bogotá (capital of Colombia) 31 C3
Bolivia (South America) 31 D5
Bolton (town in England) 19 C3
Bombay (city in India) 25 J7
Bonn (capital of West Germany) 23 L6
Bordeaux (town in France) 23 K7
Borneo (island in Asia) 25 N9
Boston (city in Massachusetts, U.S.A.) 29 L4

Bothnia, Gulf of (Europe) 23 N4
Botswana (Africa) 27 E7
Boulogne (town in France) 18 E4
Bounty I. (island in the Pacific Ocean) 40 B8
Bournemouth (town in England) 18 D4
Bouvet I. (island in Atlantic Ocean) 41 J8
Boyne (river in Ireland) 21 C3
Bradford (town in England) 19 C3
Brahmaputra Major river in Asia. Rises in 25 L6 SW Tibet and flows S into N India and Bangladesh where it merges with the Ganges delta.
Brasilia (capital of Brazil) 31 F5
Brazil (South America) 31 E5
Brazilian Highlands (South America) 31 F5
Brazzaville (capital of Congo) 27 D5
Brighton (town in England) 18 D4
Brisbane (city in Australia) 33 E5
Bristol (city in England) 18 C4
Bristol Channel (England/Wales) 18 B4
Brittany (region of France) 23 J7
Brunei (Asia) 25 N8
Brussels (capital of Belgium) 23 K6
Bucharest (capital of Romania) 23 P8
Budapest (capital of Hungary) 23 N7
Buenos Aires (capital of Argentina) 31 E7
Bujumbura (capital of Burundi) 27 E5
Bulgaria (Europe) 23 O8
Burma (Asia) 25 L6
Burundi (Africa) 27 E5
Bute (island in Scotland) 20 B2
Byrd land (region of Antarctica) 34 L

C

Cabinda (territory of Angola) 27 D5
Caernarfon (town in Wales) 19 B3
Cairngorms (mountains in Scotland) 20 C2
Cairo (capital of Egypt) 27 E2
Calcutta (city in India) 25 K6
Calgary (town in Alberta, Canada) 29 G3
Cambodia (Asia) 25 M7
Cambrian Mountains (Wales) 18 C4
Cambridge (city in England) 18 E3
Cameroon (Africa) 27 D4
Campbell I. (island in S. Pacific Ocean) 41 O8
Canada (North America) 29 G3
Canary Islands (Spanish island group) 27 A2
Canaveral, Cape (Florida, U.S.A.) 29 K6
Canberra (capital of Australia) 33 D6
Canton (city in China) 25 N6
Cape Horn (headland at the extreme S of 31 D9 South America)
Cape Town (joint capital, with Pretoria, of 27 D8 South Africa)
Cape Verde Islands (volcanic islands in 40 H5 Atlantic Ocean)
Caracas (capital of Venezuela) 31 D2
Cardiff (capital of Wales) 18 C4
Cardigan Bay (Wales) 18 B3
Caribbean Sea 29 L7
Carlisle (city in England) 19 C2
Caroline Is. (group of islands in Micronesia) 33 D2
Carpathians (mountain range in Europe) 23 O7
Carrauntoohill (mountain in Ireland) 21 B3
Casablanca (city in Morocco) 27 B1
Caspian Sea 25 F4
Castlebar (town in Rep. of Ireland) 21 B3
Caucasus (mountain range in U.S.S.R.) 25 F4
Cavan (town in Rep. of Ireland) 21 C2
Cayenne (capital of French Guiana) 31 E3
Celtic Sea 17 B3
Central African Republic (Africa) 27 D4
Central America (area of North America 38 D3 from Mexico to Colombia)

Iran (Asia) 25 G5
Iraq (Asia) 27 G1
Irish Sea 17 B3
Irkutsk (town in U.S.S.R.) 41 M3
Irrawaddy, R. Flows through Burma to 25 L6
Bay of Bengal. Important trade artery 2000 km (1250 miles) long. Navigable as far as Bhamo.
Irtysh, R. Flows N. across Siberian Plain 41 L3
to Ob R. and Arctic Ocean; 4422 km (2745 miles)
Islamabad (capital of Pakistan) 25 J5
Islay (island on W. coast Scot.) 20 A3
Israel (Asia) 27 F1
Istanbul (city in Turkey) 23 P8
Italy (Europe) 23 M8
Ivory Coast (Africa) 27 B4

J

Jakarta (capital of Indonesia) 25 M9
Jamaica (island in the Caribbean Sea) 29 L7
Jan Mayen (Norwegian island in the 40 H2
Arctic Ocean)
Japan (Asia) 25 P5
Japan, Sea of 25 P4
Java (island in Indonesia) 25 M9
Java Sea 25 N9
Jersey (island in the Channel Is.) 18 C5
Jerusalem (town in Asia) 27 F1
Johannesburg (city in South Africa) 27 E7
John O'Groats (most northerly point of 20 C1
Scottish mainland)
Jordan (Asia) 27 F1
Jura (island on W. coast Scot.) 20 B2

K

Kabul (capital of Afghanistan) 25 H5
Kalahari Desert (Africa) 27 E7
Kalgoorlie (town in Western Australia) 33 B6
Kamchatka (peninsula in U.S.S.R.) 25 S3
Kampala (capital of Uganda) 27 F4
Kanpur (city in India) 41 L4
Kara Kum (desert in Asia) 25 G4
Kara Sea 25 G1
Karachi (city in Pakistan) 25 H6
Kashmir (state in Asia) 25 J5
Katmandu (capital of Nepal) 25 K6
Kenya (Africa) 27 F4
Kerguelen I. (island in the Indian Ocean) 41 L8
Kermadec Is. (volcanic islands in 40 C7
Pacific Ocean)
Keswick (town in England) 19 C2
Khabarovsk (town in U.S.S.R.) 41 N3
Kharkov (city in Soviet Union) 23 R7
Khartoum (capital of Sudan) 27 F3
Kiev (city in the Soviet Union) 23 Q6
Kigali (capital of Rwanda) 27 E5
Kilimanjaro, Mount (highest mountain in 27 F5
Africa)
Killarney (town in Rep. of Ireland) 21 B3
Kingston (capital of Jamaica) 29 L7
Kinshasa (capital of Zaire) 27 D5
Kintyre, Mull of (peninsula in Scotland) 20 B3
Kirghiz Steppe (plains of Russia) 25 G3
Kiribati (coral islands in Micronesia) 33 G2
Kirkwall (capital of Orkney, Scotland) 20 C1
Kita-Kyushu (city in Japan) 41 N4
Kobe (city in Japan) 41 N4
Kola Peninsula (Soviet Union) 23 Q3
Kolyma River in N.E. U.S.S.R. 41 O2
Rises in Kolyma Mts. and flows N. to the Arctic Ocean. Gold mined along its course.
Kuala Lumpur (capital of Malaysia) 25 M8
Kunlun Shan (mountain range in Asia) 25 K5
Kuril Is. (chain of islands in U.S.S.R.) 41 N3
Kuwait (Asia) 27 G2
Kuwait (capital of Kuwait) 27 G2
Kuybyshev (town in U.S.S.R.) 41 K3
Kuybyshev (city in Soviet Union) 23 U6
Kwangchow (city in China) 41 M4
Kyoto (town in Japan) 41 N4

L

La Paz (capital of Bolivia) 31 D5
Labrador (region of Canada) 29 L3
Laccadive Islands (India) 25 J7
Ladoga, Lake (Soviet Union) 23 Q4
Lagan (river in Ireland) 21 C2
Lagos (capital of Nigeria) 27 C4
Lahore (city in Pakistan) 41 L4
Land's End (headland in England) 18 B4
Laos (Asia) 25 M6
Lapland (region of Europe) 23 N3
Laptev Sea 41 L2
Larne (town in Northern Ireland) 21 D2

Le Havre (seaport in France) 18 E5
Lebanon (Asia) 27 F1
Leeds (city in England) 19 D3
Leicester (town in England) 18 D3
Lena (river in Soviet Union) 25 O2
Leningrad (city in Soviet Union) 23 Q5
Lerwick (town in Shetland) 20 E1
Lesotho (Africa) 27 E7
Lewis (island in the Hebrides) 20 A1
Lhasa (city in Tibet) 41 M4
Liberia (Africa) 27 B4
Libreville (capital of Gabon) 27 C4
Libya (Africa) 27 D2
Lilongwe (capital of Malawi) 27 F6
Limerick (city in Rep. of Ireland) 21 B3
Lisbon (capital of Portugal) 22 H9
Liverpool (city in England) 19 C3
Lizard Pt. (headland in England) 18 B5
Llanos (plains of South America) 31 C3
Lofoten (island chain in Norway) 23 M3
Loire River in central France. 23 J7
Longest river in the country. Popular tourist area - châteaux, vineyards.
Lomé (capital of Togo) 27 C4
Lomond, Loch (Scotland) 20 B2
London (capital of United Kingdom) 18 D4
Londonderry (city in Northern Ireland) 21 C2
Los Angeles (city in California, U.S.A.) 29 G5
Lower California (peninsula of Mexico) 29 G5
Luanda (capital of Angola) 27 D5
Lusaka (capital of Zambia) 27 E6
Lüta (town in China) 41 N4
Luton (town in England) 18 D4
Luxembourg (Europe) 23 L7

M

Macao (Portuguese colony in Asia) 25 N6
McDonald Is. (islands in the Indian Ocean) 41 L8
Mackenzie R. River in North West Territories, 29 F2
Canada. With Slave, Peace and Finlay rivers, forms a waterway navigable from the N.W. Arctic coast 3200 kms (2000 miles) inland. Mineral resources in valley.
McKinley, Mount (Highest mountain in 29 D2
North America)
Macquarie I. (group of islands in Pacific 41 O8
Ocean)
Madagascar (island in the Indian Ocean) 27 G7
Madeira (Portuguese island group) 27 A1
Madeira, R. River in N.W. Brazil 31 C4
Tributary of the Amazon which it joins 85 m E. of Manaus
Madras (city in India) 25 J7
Madrid (capital of Spain) 22 J8
Magadan (town in U.S.S.R.) 41 N2
Magellan, Strait of (separating mainland 31 C9
South America and Tierra del Fuego)
Magnitogorsk (town in the Soviet Union) 25 G3
Majorca (Spanish island in the Mediterranean) 23 K9
Malabo (capital of Equatorial Guinea) 27 C4
Malacca, Strait of (channel between Malay 25 L8
peninsula and Sumatra)
Malawi (Africa) 27 F6
Malaysia (Asia) 25 M8
Maldives (island group in Asia) 25 J8
Mali (Africa) 27 B3
Malin Head (most northerly point in Ireland) 21 C2
Malta (Europe) 23 M9
Man, Isle of (island in the Irish Sea) 19 B2
Managua (capital of Nicaragua) 29 K7
Manaus (city in Brazil) 31 D4
Manchester (city in England) 19 C3
Manchuria (region of China) 25 N4
Manilla (capital of the Philippines) 25 O7
Maputo (capital of Mozambique) 27 F7
Maranón, R. Rises in the Andes in W. Peru. 31 C4
Flows N. in Peru and bends E. to join Ucayali R. to form the Amazon.
Margate (town in England) 18 E4
Mariana Islands (group of islands in the 33 D1
Pacific Ocean)
Marquesas Is. (volcanic islands in 40 D6
Pacific Ocean)
Marseille (city in France) 23 L8
Marshall Islands (coral islands in the 33 G2
Pacific Ocean)
Maseru (capital of Lesotho) 27 E7
Mato Grosso (plateau region in Brazil) 31 E5
Mauritania (Africa) 27 A2
Mauritius (island in the Indian Ocean) 27 H6
Mbabane (capital of Swaziland) 27 F7
Mecca (Holy city of Islam, Saudi Arabia) 27 F2
Medellin (city in Colombia) 31 C3
Mediterranean Sea 23 N10
Mekong R. Rises in Tibet, flows to 25 M7
S. China Sea. Longest in Asia 4500 km (2800 miles) long.

Melanesia (region of islands in Pacific Ocean) 39 N4
Melbourne (city in Australia) 33 D6
Melville Is. (island in Canada) 40 E1
Mexico (North America) 29 H6
Mexico City (capital of Mexico) 29 J7
Mexico, Gulf of 29 J6
Miami (city in Florida, U.S.A.) 29 K6
Michigan, L. (one of the Great Lakes, 29 J4
North America)
Micronesia (region of islands in the Pacific 39 N3
Ocean)
Middlesbrough (town in England) 19 D2
Milan (city in Italy) 23 L7
Milford Haven (town in Wales) 18 B4
Minch, The (channel between Hebrides and 20 A2
mainland Scotland)
Minneapolis (city in U.S.A.) 40 E3
Mississippi River in central U.S.A. 29 J5
Rises in N.W. Minnesota and flows 3600 km (2300 miles) to G. of Mexico near New Orleans. Drains over 2 500 000 sq. km. Liable to flood.
Missouri, R. River in North America. 29 H4
Major tributary of Mississippi that joins near St. Louis. Length 3800 km (2400 miles) H.E.P. irrigation schemes. Source found by Lewis and Clark.
Mizen Head (headland in Ireland) 21 B4
Mogadishu (capital of Somalia) 27 G4
Mombasa (city in Kenya) 27 F5
Monaco (Europe) 23 L8
Mongolia (Asia) 25 L4
Monrovia (capital of Liberia) 27 A4
Mont Blanc (Highest mountain in the Alps) 23 L7
Monterrey (city in Mexico) 40 E4
Montevideo (capital of Uruguay) 31 E7
Montreal (city in Canada) 29 L4
Moray Firth (inlet in N. Scotland) 20 C2
Morecambe (town in England) 19 C2
Morocco (Africa) 27 A1
Moscow (capital of the Soviet Union) 23 R5
Mount Cook (highest in New Zealand) 33 F7
Mourne Mountain (Ireland) 21 C2
Mozambique (Africa) 27 F7
Mozambique Channel 27 F6
Mull (island on W. coast Scot.) 20 B2
Murmansk (town in Soviet Union) 41 K2
Murray, R. River in S.E. Australia. 33 D6
Rises in Australian Alps and flows W. to L. Alexandrina and the sea. Longest river in the country. With its tributaries Darling, Murrumbidgee, Lachlan it is extensively used for irrigation and H.E.P. Over 2500 km (1600 miles) long.
Muscat (capital of Oman) 27 H2

N

Nagasaki (city in Japan) 25 O5
Nagoya (city in Japan) 41 N4
Nairobi (capital of Kenya) 27 F5
Namibia (Africa) 27 D7
Nan Ling (mountain range in China) 25 M6
Nanking (town in China) 41 M4
Naples (city in Italy) 23 M8
Nassau (capital of the Bahamas) 29 L6
Nasser, Lake (Africa) 27 F2
Nauru (coral island in Micronesia) 33 F3
N'Djamena (capital of Chad) 27 D3
Neagh, Lough (Ireland) 21 C2
Nepal (Asia) 25 K6
Ness, Loch (Scotland) 20 B2
Netherlands (Europe) 23 K6
New Amsterdam (island in the Indian Ocean) 41 L7
New Caledonia (volcanic island in Pacific 33 F5
Ocean)
New Delhi (capital of India) 25 J6
New Forest (England) 18 D4
New Guinea (island in the Pacific) 33 C3
New Orleans (city in Louisiana, U.S.A.) 29 K6
New Siberian Islands (U.S.S.R.) 25 O1
New South Wales (state in Australia) 33 D6
New York (largest city in U.S.A.) 29 L4
New Zealand (island in the Pacific Ocean) 33 F6
Newcastle (city in England) 19 D2
Newfoundland (island in Canada) 29 N4
Newport (town in Wales) 18 C4
Newry (town in Ireland) 21 C2
Niagara Falls (waterfalls on Niagara R. 29 L4
North America)
Niamey (capital of Niger) 27 C3
Nicaragua (Central America) 29 K7
Nicobar Islands (India) 25 L8
Nicosia (capital of Cyprus) 23 Q9
Niger (Africa) 27 C3
Niger, R. River in Africa. 4100 km (2600 miles) 27 C4
long. Navigable for 1600 km (1000 miles). Major waterway, explored by Mungo Park, 1796. Many rapids, swamps and sand bars.
Nigeria (Africa) 27 C3

Nile River in N.E. Africa. The world's **27 F2**
longest river; 6671 km (4145 miles). Dams now
control its annual flooding and provide H.E.P. and
irrigation. Site of several early civilisations.

Nile Delta (mouth of the Nile R.) **23 Q10**
Norilsk (town in U.S.S.R.) **41 L2**
North America (continent) **38 D2**
North Cape (Norway) **23 P2**
North Channel (Ireland/Scotland) **21 C2**
North Dvina River in N.W. U.S.S.R. **23 S4**
Flows to the White Sea at Arkhangel'sk where
it forms a delta.
North Island (New Zealand) **33 G6**
North Korea (Asia) **25 O4**
North Pole (northern end of the earth's axis) **34 R**
North Sea **23 K5**
North West Cape (Australia) **33 A5**
North West Highlands (mountains in **20 B2**
Scotland)
North York Moors (England) **19 D2**
Northampton (town in England) **18 D3**
Northern Ireland (United Kingdom) **21 C2**
Northern Territory (Australia) **33 C4**
Norway (Europe) **23 L4**
Norwegian Sea **23 J3**
Norwich (city in England) **18 E3**
Nottingham (city in England) **19 D3**
Nouakchott (capital of Mauritania) **27 A3**
Novaya Zemlya (group of Russian islands) **25 F1**
Novosibirsk (city in Soviet Union) **25 K3**
Nyasa, Lake (Africa) **27 F6**

O

Ob (river in the Soviet Union) **25 H2**
Oban (town in Scotland) **20 B2**
Oder Rises in N. Central Czechoslovakia **23 N6**
flows N.E. through Poland to enter Baltic Sea.
Odessa (city in the Soviet Union) **23 Q7**
Ohio, R. E. U.S.A. Principal tributary of **29 K5**
Mississippi R. 1576 km (980 m) long. Flood control
by dams and reservoirs.
Okhotsk, Sea of **25 Q3**
Omagh (town in Northern Ireland) **21 C2**
Oman (Asia) **27 H3**
Oman, Gulf of **25 G6**
Omsk (city in U.S.S.R.) **41 L3**
Onega, Lake (Soviet Union) **23 R4**
Orange, R. River in Africa. Flows 2080 km **27 D4**
(1300 miles) W. from Drakensburg to the Atlantic
Ocean. Forms S. boundary of Namibia (S.W. Africa).
Numerous irrigation and H.E.P. dams.
Orinoco, R. River in South America. **31 D3**
Rises in Sierra Parima, flows 2700 km (1700 miles)
through Venezuela to Atlantic Ocean.
Orkney (island group, Scotland) **20 C1**
Osaka (city in Japan) **25 P5**
Oslo (capital of Norway) **23 M4**
Ottawa (capital of Canada) **29 L4**
Ouagadougou (capital of Upper Volta) **27 B3**
Ouse (river in England) **18 E3**
Oxford (city in England) **18 D4**

P

Pacific Ocean **38 B3**
Pakistan (Asia) **25 H6**
Palembang (city in Indonesia) **41 M6**
Pampas (plains in Argentina) **31 D7**
Panamá (Central America) **29 L8**
Panamá (capital of Panamá) **29 L8**
Panamá Canal (ship canal connecting **29 L8**
Atlantic to Pacific)
Papua New Guinea (New Guinea) **33 D3**
Paraguay (South America) **31 E6**
Paramaribo (capital of Surinam) **31 E3**
Paris (capital of France) **23 K7**
Parry Is. (group of islands in Canada) **40 E1**
Patagonia (plateau region of Argentina) **31 C8**
Peebles (town in Scotland) **20 C3**
Peking (capital of China) **25 N4**
Pennines (mountains in England) **19 C2**
Pentland Firth (strait between Orkney and **20 C1**
N. Scotland)
Perth (city in Australia) **33 A6**
Perth (town in Scotland) **20 C2**
Peru (South America) **31 C5**
Peterborough (city in England) **18 E3**
Peterhead (town in Scotland) **20 D2**
Petropavlovsk-Kamchatskiy (town in **41 O3**
U.S.S.R.)
Philadelphia (city in Pennsylvania, U.S.A.) **29 L4**
Philippines (Asia) **25 N7**
Phnom Penh (capital of Cambodia) **25 M7**
Phoenix Is. (coral islands in the Pacific Ocean) **40 C6**
Pitcairn Is. (volcanic island in the Pacific **40 D7**
Ocean)

Plymouth (city in England) **18 B4**
Poland (Europe) **23 N6**
Polynesia (region of islands in the Pacific **38 A3**
Ocean)
Port-au-Prince (capital of Haiti) **29 L7**
Port Elizabeth (town in South Africa) **27 E8**
Port Moresby (capital of Papua New Guinea) **33 D3**
Portland Bill (headland in England) **18 C4**
Porto Novo (capital of Benin) **27 C4**
Portrush (town in Northern Ireland) **21 C2**
Portsmouth (city in England) **18 D4**
Portugal (Europe) **22 H8**
Prague (capital of Czechoslovakia) **23 M7**
Prairies (fertile plains of North America) **29 G3**
Pretoria (administrative capital of South Africa) **27 E7**
Prince Edward Is. (islands in the Indian **41 K8**
Ocean)
Puerto Montt (city in Chile) **31 C8**
Puerto Rico (island in the West Indies) **40 F5**
Putumayo, R. Rises in Colombian Andes and **31 C4**
flows S.E. to join the Amazon in Brazil. Forms much
of Peru - Colombia boundary.
Pyongyang (capital of North Korea) **25 O5**
Pyrenees (mountain range between France **23 J8**
and Spain)

Q

Qatar (Asia) **27 H2**
Quebec (capital of Quebec, Canada) **29 L4**
Queen Elizabeth Is. (Canada) **29 G1**
Queen Maud Land (section of Antarctica) **34 C**
Queensland (state in Australia) **33 D5**
Quezon City (city in the Philippines) **41 N5**
Quito (capital of Ecuador) **31 C3**

R

Rabat (capital of Morocco) **27 B1**
Rangoon (capital of Burma) **25 L7**
Rathlin Island (Ireland) **21 C2**
Reading (town in England) **18 D4**
Recife (city in Brazil) **31 G4**
Red Sea **27 F2**
Ree, Lough (Ireland) **21 C3**
Republic of Ireland (Europe) **21 B3**
Réunion (island in the Indian Ocean) **27 H7**
Reykjavik (capital of Iceland) **22 E4**
Rhine River in Europe. Rises in Switzerland **23 L7**
flows N.W. through Germany and Netherlands to
North Sea at Rotterdam. Many vineyards along
banks. Major transportation route.
Rhodes (Greek island in the Aegean) **23 P9**
Rhodesia see Zimbabwe
Rhône River in Europe. Rises in Switzerland **23 K8**
and flows through E. France to G. of Lions. Fast
flow harnessed to power production.
Rio de Janeiro (city in Brazil) **31 F6**
Rio de la Plata (estuary of the Paraná and **31 E7**
Uruguay rivers)
Rio Grande River in North America. **29 H6**
Flows 3034 km (1885 miles) from S.W. Colorado to
G. of Mexico at Brownsville. Forms the U.S.-Mexican
border for much of its length.
Rio Negro River in N. Brazil. Rises in **31 D4**
E. Colombia and flows E. and S.E. to join the
Amazon. Forms part of Colombia-Venezuela border.
Riyadh (capital of Saudi Arabia) **27 G2**
Rocky Mountains (North America) **29 F3**
Romania (Europe) **23 O7**
Rome (capital of Italy) **23 M8**
Rosario (city in Argentina) **40 F7**
Ross Sea **34 J**
Rostov (city in the Soviet Union) **23 R7**
Rouen (town in France) **18 E5**
Rub Al Khali (desert region in the Arabian **27 G3**
peninsula)
Rudolf, Lake (Africa) **27 F4**
Rum (island in the Hebrides) **20 A2**
Rwanda (Africa) **27 E5**
Ryukyu Is. (chain of islands of Japan) **41 N4**

S

St. Andrews (town in Scotland) **20 C2**
St. George's Channel (Ireland/Wales) **21 C4**
St. Helena (island in the Atlantic Ocean) **40 H6**
St. Ives (town in England) **18 B4**
St. John's (capital of Newfoundland, Canada) **29 N4**
St. Lawrence, R. River and seaway in **29 L4**
North America. Rises in Minnesota and flows
through the Great Lakes and on to the Gulf of
St. Lawrence. Major waterway for ocean-going
vessels carrying oil, grain, timber, iron ore. Navigable
for 3000 km (1864 miles).

St. Louis (city in U.S.A.) **40 E4**
St. Lucia (island in the West Indies) **31 D2**
St. Paul (island in the Indian Ocean) **41 L7**
St. Vincent (island in the West Indies) **31 D2**
Sahara (desert in Africa) **27 B2**
Sakhalin (island in Soviet Union) **25 Q3**
Salisbury Plain (England) **18 C4**
Salt Lake City (city in U.S.A.) **40 E3**
Salvador (city in Brazil) **31 G5**
San Francisco (city in California, U.S.A.) **29 F5**
San José (capital of Costa Rica) **29 K7**
San Marino (Republic in Italy) **23 M8**
San Salvador (capital of El Salvador) **29 K7**
Sana (capital of Yemen) **27 G3**
Santiago (capital of Chile) **31 C6**
Santo Domingo (capital of Dominican **29 M7**
Republic)
Sao Paolo (city in Brazil) **31 F6**
São Tomé and Principe (group of African **27 C4**
islands)
Sapporo (town in Japan) **41 N3**
Sardinia (Italian island in the Mediterranean) **23 L8**
Sark (island in the Channel Is.) **18 C5**
Saskatoon (city in Saskatchewan, Canada) **29 H3**
Saudi Arabia (Asia) **27 G2**
Scafell Pike (mountain in England) **19 C2**
Scarborough (town in England) **19 D2**
Scilly, Isles of (England) **18 A5**
Scotland (United Kingdom) **17 C2**
Seattle (Largest city in Washington, U.S.A.) **29 F4**
Seine, R. Rises in Plateau of Langres in France **23 K7**
and flows N.W. across the Paris Basin to enter
the English Channel near Le Havre. Navigable as far
as Rouen.
Selvas (forested region of the Amazon Basin) **31 C4**
Senegal (Africa) **27 A3**
Sénégal, R. River in Africa. Flows N.W. **27 A3**
and W. from central Guinea to the Atlantic, north of
Cape Verde. Fertile in upper reaches. 1600 km
(1000 miles) long.
Seoul (capital of South Korea) **25 O5**
Severn (river in England/Wales) **18 C3**
Severnaya Zemlya (group of Russian islands) **25 L1**
Shanghai (city in China) **25 O5**
Shannon (largest river in Ireland) **21 B3**
Sheffield (city in England) **19 D3**
Shenyang (city in China) **25 O4**
Shetland (island group, Scotland) **20 E1**
Sian (town in China) **41 M4**
Siberia (region of U.S.S.R.) **25 J2**
Sicily (island and region of Italy) **23 M9**
Sierra Leone (Africa) **27 A4**
Sierra Nevada (mountain range in North **29 F5**
America)
Sierra Nevada (mountain range in Spain) **22 H9**
Sinai (peninsula in Africa) **27 F2**
Singapore (Asia) **25 M8**
Skagerrak (strait between Norway and **23 L5**
Denmark)
Skye (island in the Hebrides) **20 A2**
Sligo (town in Rep. of Ireland) **21 B2**
Snowdon, Mount (highest mt. in England **19 B3**
or Wales)
Socotra (island in the Indian Ocean) **27 H3**
Sofia (capital of Bulgaria) **23 O8**
Solomon Is. (islands in Melanesia) **33 E3**
Solway Firth (England/Scotland) **19 C2**
Somalia (Africa) **27 G4**
South Africa (Africa) **27 E8**
South America (continent) **38 E4**
South Australia (state in Australia) **33 C5**
South China Sea **25 M8**
South Georgia (island in the South Atlantic) **31 G9**
South Island (New Zealand) **33 F7**
South Korea (Asia) **25 O5**
South Orkney Is. (islands in the Atlantic **40 G8**
Ocean)
South Pole (southern end of the earth's axis) **34 E**
South Sandwich Is. (volcanic islands in the **40 H8**
Atlantic)
South Shetland Is. (island group in the **40 G9**
S. Atlantic)
South West Africa see Namibia
South Yemen (Asia) **27 G3**
Southampton (town in England) **18 D4**
Southend (town in England) **18 E4**
Southern Ocean **34 D**
Southern Uplands (Scotland) **20 B3**
Southport (town in England) **19 C3**
Soviet Union (Asia) **25 G3**
Spain (Europe) **22 H9**
Spey (river in Scotland) **20 C2**
Spitsbergen (group of Norwegian islands) **25 C1**
Sri Lanka (Asia) **25 K8**
Stanley (capital of the Falkland Islands) **31 E9**
Stanley Falls (waterfalls on Zaire R., Africa) **27 E4**
Stanovoy Mountains (Soviet Union) **25 N3**
Stirling (town in Scotland) **20 B2**
Stockholm (capital of Sweden) **23 N5**